Teddy And His Constant Companions

By Celia Baham

On the cover: Hare Extraordinaire,
Cat, and Dog. Photo by Steve Baham.

Additional copies of this book may be purchased
at http://www.CeliasTeddies.com

©2005 by Celia Baham.

All rights reserved. No part of this book may be reproduced or utilized in
any form or by any means, electronic or mechanical, including photocopy
ing, recording, or by any information storage and retrieval system, without
permission in writing from the Publisher. Inquiries should be addressed to
Celia Baham by emailing celia@celiasteddies.com.

Printed in the United States of America

TABLE OF CONTENTS

ACKNOWLEDGMENTS / 5

ABOUT THE AUTHOR / 5

INTRODUCTION / 7

BASIC DIRECTIONS / 9

BEAR / 17

CAROUSEL HORSE / 33

CAT / 45

DOG / 57

ELEPHANT / 63

GIRAFFE / 69

HARE EXTRAORDINAIRE / 75

HEDGEHOG / 89

MONKEY / 93

MOUSE / 103

PANDA / 111

RAT / 123

SOURCES / 129

ACKNOWLEDGMENTS

I am very grateful to my husband for all his help in producing this book. He has been my sounding board and has allowed me all the time to design. With his computer skills, he put this book on disk and he has been my proofreader.

I also want to thank the collectors and students of my classes. I take great joy in teaching and developing new artists.

ABOUT THE AUTHOR

In a small home in big Silicon Valley (San Jose, California) lives Celia Baham with her husband, Steve. Their home has vignettes – in practically every corner of every room – of her creations and the many bears she has collected over the past twenty five years.

Celia divides her time between serving others and making her own designs. She has: been a regular worker and an oil painter; had a stained glass business; sold dolls; and run an export business. Celia enjoys being around people – she loves to cook for large groups. She enjoys sharing her craft with others, especially young children. She takes a sample of her bear collection to elementary schools to show and discuss how they are made.

Celia has designed many bear patterns for Teddy Bear Review and Soft Cloth Dolls & Animals; has designed bears for L.L. Knickerbocker and Little World of Miniatures; and has designed her own line as well. On cable television, she has demonstrated how to make a bear and has traveled extensively throughout the United States, England and Canada, teaching the craft to others. For the past few years, she has been a regular workshop teacher at the John C. Campbell Folk School in North Carolina. She has several pieces on exhibit in the Teddy Bear Museum in Naples, Florida, and in Tokyo, Japan. Her first book, *Costumed Teddy Bears: 14 Bears in Body Suits*, contains fourteen of her most innovative Teddy Bear designs.

Over the past two decades of her career in bear artistry, she has won well over one hundred awards and ribbons. She has been a judge several times for the *Teddy Bear & Friends* Toby Awards and has twice been nominated for the prestigious Golden Teddy Award, winning once. Other honors include the International Doll Exchange "Most Popular Bear" and numerous regional First Place and Best of Show awards.

Celia's bears have been photographed by well known photographer Ron Kimball and appear frequently on calendars, bookmarks, puzzles and even a teachers' poster. Her inspirations are books, greeting cards and life itself! She has donated bears to many charitable organizations including cancer research, Kobe, Japan, children's relief, Good Bears of the World and the Ronald McDonald House.

Now a grandmother, you can be sure Celia's grand children will never be without a special furry friend!

INTRODUCTION

I love teddy bears! I have enjoyed designing and making teddy bears for over twenty years – no, make that thirty years (how time flies!) – ever since my children were small. Now I get to "start over" with the grandchildren! Though only toys today ("Now, be careful with Teddy!"), I know they are sure to be treasured keepsakes for generations to come.

In my travels, I have been inspired to design "furry friends" for my bear collection. This book has some of my favorites.

The Carousel Horse was specially designed to hold a small bear. However, with or without a rider, he is very impressive.

The Cat was created after seeing the play "Cats" in London. I loved the costumes and this pattern is my interpretation.

And Hare Extraordinaire. What a character! All formal in tie and tails, looking quite debonair, he reminds me of hotel doormen we saw in Europe.

I saw a Hedgehog in Germany. Sooo cute! He is very simple to make and would make a great accessory for a gift package.

The Rat was popular in some European shows I attended. I cannot quite figure out why. Nevertheless, this Rat was designed for New York's Toy Fair. He is made to be posed seated, and is so sassy.

Some of these patterns are simple, while some are a challenge. All make unique "furry friends." Please enjoy making them as much as I do!

Celia Baham
Celia's Teddies

BASIC DIRECTIONS

Fabrics:

Mohair is one of the most widely used fabrics in making collectible animals. Mohair comes in a wide variety of colors and textures but is rather expensive.

European synthetic furs have become very sought after in the past few years. The fabric is man made but woven just like mohair and is easy to work with. See **Sources**.

Recycled fur can also be used. Buy secondhand garments. Dismantle coats, capes or collars and discard the lining. Since real fur can stretch, line the fur with muslin before cutting pattern pieces.

Wool coats make great animals. *Hare Extraordinaire* is made from wool and dressed in felt. Dismantle the wool coat and wash in hot water. Dry in a hot dryer to make the wool felt like.

Wool felt works well for paws and sole pads as well as clothes. See **Sources**.

Pile is the furry side of the material and comes in different lengths and thicknesses.

Nap is the direction in which the fur lies flat. The arrows on the pattern pieces tell in which direction the nap should be oriented.

Dye: Always wash fabrics after dyeing to check for bleeding of the dye. This is very important in mixing fabrics. You would not want to spend lots of time and effort creating an animal just to be disappointed by bleeding dye colors.

Patterns:

Make permanent patterns: Do not cut patterns out of the book. Instead, trace the pattern onto tracing paper, cut out the pattern and trace the pattern pieces onto cardboard. Cereal box cardboard works well, as do the plastic sheets that quilters use.

Mark the pattern pieces: Always put all the pattern markings on the permanent pattern pieces as well as the name of the bear or animal. It will save a lot of trouble if the pieces ever happen to get mixed up! Be sure to mark "left and right" on the pattern pieces that are to be cut in reverse.

Lay out the pattern on the fabric: Trace all of the pattern pieces on the back of the fabric. A suggested pattern layout is shown for each animal. If the material has a dark backing, use a white oil pencil (seamstress pencil). Pieces marked "Cut 2 (or 4), 1 (or 2) in reverse," indicates there are "left and right" pieces. Always flip the pattern over and check the nap arrows to match the direction. It is a good idea to place all of the pattern pieces (including all the reverse pieces) on the fabric before starting to cut, just to make sure you have enough material for the project.

Cutting and Sewing:

<u>Cut out the pieces:</u> When cutting fur with a pile, keep the scissors blade on the "fur" side, close against the backing, being very careful not to cut the pile.

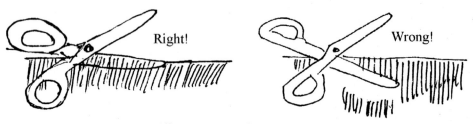

Illustration 1. Cutting Fur

Save the scraps. Even the smallest scraps can be used for stuffing larger animals, thus using up all those expensive fabrics!

<u>Sew the pieces:</u> Read all the instructions before sewing the pieces together. Always double check the diagrams to make sure you are sewing the seams correctly. It is no fun ripping them out and starting over!

I recommend using #16 and #15 needles for sewing fur. Use beige thread with lighter color furs. If the fabric frays easily, use a product that prevents fraying before sewing. Lock the stitches at the end of seams. With fur with longer pile, use a wider stitch.

Most seam allowances are about 1/4 inch (.65cm). When sewing curves, fabrics tend to stretch, so pinning curved pieces together before sewing is advisable. For animal heads, baste the head gusset to the side head piece before machine sewing, in order to prevent stretching.

All seams should be combed before turning the pieces right side out. Spread the edges of the seam apart and comb out the fur. The seam will look neater and lay flat.

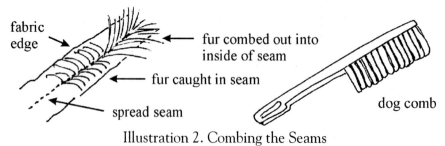

Illustration 2. Combing the Seams

Joints:

The recommended types of joints are cotter pins for smaller animals, and hex head bolts for stronger joints for larger pieces. Use 1 1/2 inch (4cm) cotter pins and bolts. Both types of joints are assembled with fender washers and fiber disks. The fiber disks are about 1/8 inch (3mm) thick with a central hole diameter of about 3/16 inch (5mm). The outer diameter depends on the size of the animal and is specified in the materials list for each pattern. Fender washers are ordinary 1/2 inch (1cm) diameter washers. The fenders prevent wear damage to the fiber disks.

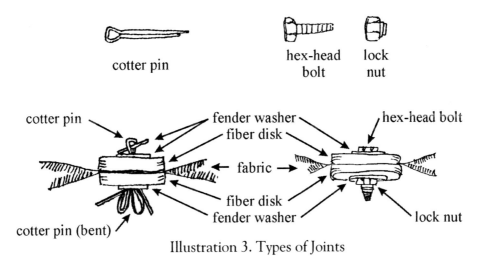

Illustration 3. Types of Joints

If commercially made fiber disks are unavailable, make your own. Draw a pattern and cut three or four disks from cereal box cardboard. Glue the layers together and set on a flat surface under some weight, perhaps a book or two, so the disk dries flat. Use an awl to make the center hole large enough for the cotter pin or bolt.

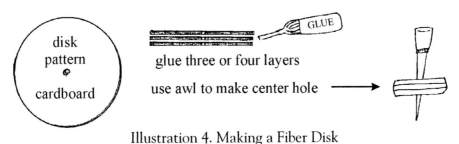

Illustration 4. Making a Fiber Disk

Assembling cotter pin joints: First spread the cotter pin and thread a fender washer on one leg. Push the washer all the way up to the loop. This is to prevent pulling the cotter pin through the joint when tightening. Close the cotter pin and thread on a fender washer and fiber disk. Make a hole with an awl in the animal limb and body at the joint location. Push the cotter pin through the limb and body fabric. On the inside of the body, thread the other fiber disk and fender washer onto the cotter pin. Use needle nose pliers to twist the legs or the cotter pin into loops. Twist the loops in opposite directions as tight as you can so the loops are tight against the washer.

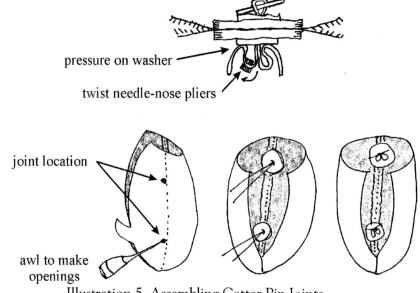

Illustration 5. Assembling Cotter Pin Joints

Assembling bolt joints: Bolt joints are more easily assembled by holding the head of the bolt with locking pliers and tightening the lock nut with another pair of pliers. If using a bolt joint for a movable head, a different method of tightening is required since the head is completed, stuffed and closed around the bolt before attaching to the body. A good method is to epoxy the bolt, fender washer and fiber disk together before installing inside the head. Let the epoxy cure hard and then complete the head. When attaching the head to the body, hold the head (and disk) while tightening the lock nut inside the body. A second method is to assemble the joint inside the body and hold the bolt with needle nose pliers up close against the fender washer. Screw the lock nut onto the bolt. Try to not let the bolt slip and damage the threads. When the nut has been screwed on as far as possible, move the needle nose pliers to the outer end of the bolt and complete tightening the nut against the fender washer.

Jointing sequence: Gather and close the neck opening tightly. Use a 1/2 inch (1cm) seam around the neck opening. Attach the completed head to the body first. Next the arms and finally the legs.

Finishing the Head:

Attach the eyes: The eyes are generally located next to the seam between the head gusset and side pieces. Experiment with moving the location until the eyes look just right. Never pierce a seam to place the eyes as this weakens the seam.

Eyes for "collector" pieces are generally made of glass. Glass eyes come with wire attached. If the wire is straight, bend the wire into a loop and twist it so the loop cannot pull loose. Attach eyes with waxed upholstery thread for strength. If the thread is too bulky for a small animal, it can be separated in up to four strands. See **Sources.**

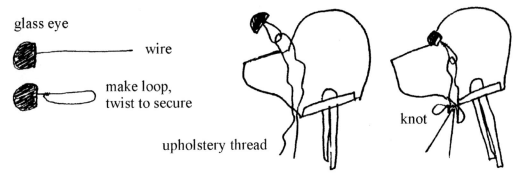

Illustration 6. Attaching Glass Eyes

Animals for children should have safety (plastic) eyes. These eyes have a plastic stem and come with a disk that locks tight onto the stem.

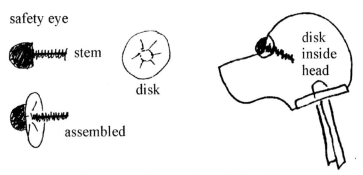

Illustration 7. Attaching Safety Eyes

<u>Attach the ears:</u> Look at the photographs for ear placement. Ears for bears are sewn on about 1/4 inch (.65cm) into the head gusset (point A in the illustration) and down the side head (point B). Cup the ear and attach the center of the ear at point C about 1/2 inch (1cm) back from points A and B. Tie a knot, bury the thread in the head and cut off. A similar technique can be applied to other animals.

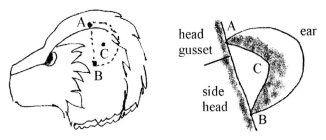

Illustration 8. Attaching Bear Ears

Shave the muzzle: Some animals look good with a shaved muzzle. First, cut the fur as short as possible with scissors. Then use a moustache trimmer to get a clean look.

Embroider the nose: Use Perlé Cotton (brand) to sew the nose and mouth. One technique for making neat and even noses is to cut a felt template in the shape of the nose and attach it to the head. Then embroider over the template with closely spaced stitches.

Or you can be creative and make a nose from a piece of leather or molded cernit.

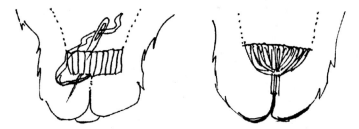

Illustration 9. Embroidering the Nose

Waxing the nose with beeswax makes it shiny. Warm the wax to soften and apply to the embroidered nose. Polish with a piece of brown paper bag (some use computer paper). Cut a strip of the paper and buff the nose until shiny. Experiment on a sample piece first.

Embroider the mouth: Attach the embroidery thread to the head at the corner of the mouth (point 1). Push the needle through the fabric from point 2 to point 3, catching the thread as shown. Pull tight and anchor at point 3. Embroider from point 3 up to the nose. If the mouth is to be curved, add additional stitching along the mouth line between points 1 and 3 and points 2 and 3 to hold the curve in place.

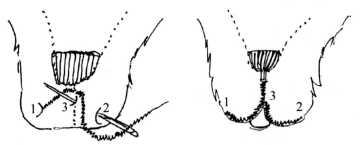

Illustration 10. Embroidering the Mouth

Stuffing and Closing:

Stuff all of the pieces: After jointing all limbs, start stuffing. Use fiberfill, excelsior or plastic pellets. Start with the body, then the arms and legs. If the animal is for children, stuff softly. Collectors, however, prefer very firmly stuffed animals.

Plastic pellets make a heavier animal. If using pellets, make small cloth pouches to hold the pellets inside the animal. Then if a seam pops, there will not be pellets all over the place! For animals in the hands of small children, I prefer not to use pellets.

For excelsior stuffing, look for the softer type of excelsior. It is much nicer on the hands!

A bamboo chopstick makes a good tool for stuffing. Sandpaper the small end to remove sharp edges that could catch on the fabric.

Close the seams: Close the seams using a ladder stitch.

Illustration 11. Closing the Seams

Close the body last in case a little extra stuffing is needed.

Painting: Paint face details (like *Hare Extraordinaire*) with acrylic paint. Dye pens can also be used, for example, to make the spots on the giraffe.

BEAR
Size: 27 inches (70cm) – Intermediate Level

MATERIALS:

1 1/4 yards (125cm) of mohair, 3/4 inch to 1 inch (2cm to 3cm) long
13 inch (33cm) square of upholstery material or 100 percent wool for paws, soles
Two 10mm or 12mm eyes, glass or plastic
Four 4 3/4 inch (12cm) diameter fiber disks for leg joints
Six 4 inch (10cm) diameter fiber disks for arm and head joints
Five 2 inch (5cm) hex head bolts with lock nuts
Fifteen 1/2 inch (1cm) fender washers for joints
Two 20 ounce bags of fiberfill
One bag of plastic pellets
Black Perlé thread for embroidering nose and mouth
Upholstery thread for attaching eyes and closing seams
Sewing machine thread to match fabric
Ribbon for bow

This diagram represents all the pieces required to complete the *Bear*, laid out on the straight of the fabric. More than one piece of fabric may be required for laying out the pattern pieces.

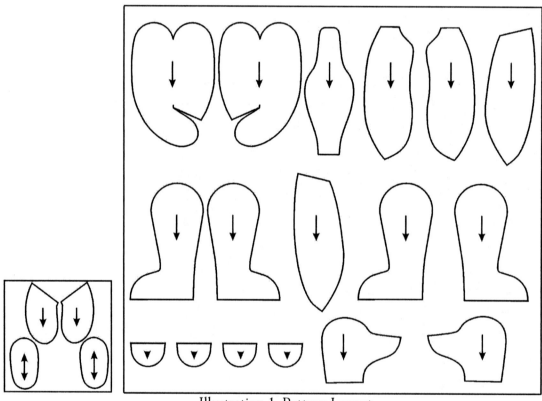

Illustration 1. Pattern Layout

INSTRUCTIONS:

Sew the two side head pieces together from the nose down to the neck edge. Sew the center head gusset to the side head pieces. Pin the gusset to the side head before sewing to keep the pieces from moving.

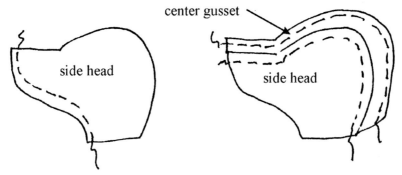

Illustration 2. Sew the Head

Sew the front and back of the ears together. Sew the bottom seam in about 1 inch (3cm) on each side to leave room for turning the ear. Turn the ears right side out.

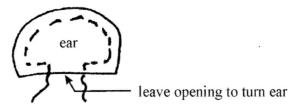

Illustration 3. Sew the Ears

Sew the front seam of the body fronts together. Sew the back seam of the body backs together, leaving an opening for stuffing. Sew the front to the back along the side seams. Leave the neck open.

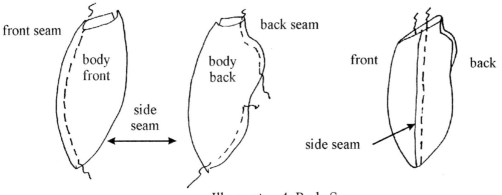

Illustration 4. Body Seams

Sew the paw to the arm. Sew the arms together, leaving the top open for stuffing.

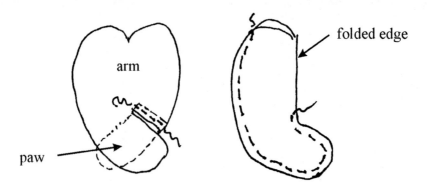

Illustration 5. Sew the Paws and Arms

Sew the legs together, leaving the top open for stuffing. Sew the soles to the legs.

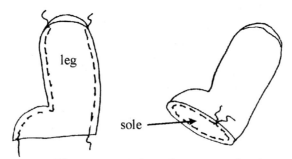

Illustration 6. Sew the Legs and Soles

Make disks for the arms (four), legs (four) and head (two, same size as arm disk). Refer to the **Basic Directions**.

Stuff the head, attach the eyes and ears, and embroider the nose and mouth. Make up one half of the head joint and close the head around the fiber disk.

Join the head to the body, then the arms and finally the legs.

Stuff the arms, legs and finally the body.

Close all seams, the body seam last, in case a little more stuffing is required.

Tie a bow around the neck.

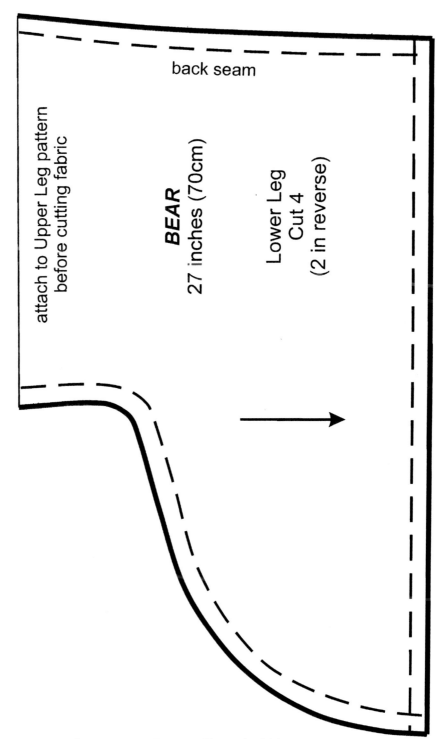

Illustration 7. Pattern Sheet 1 of 11

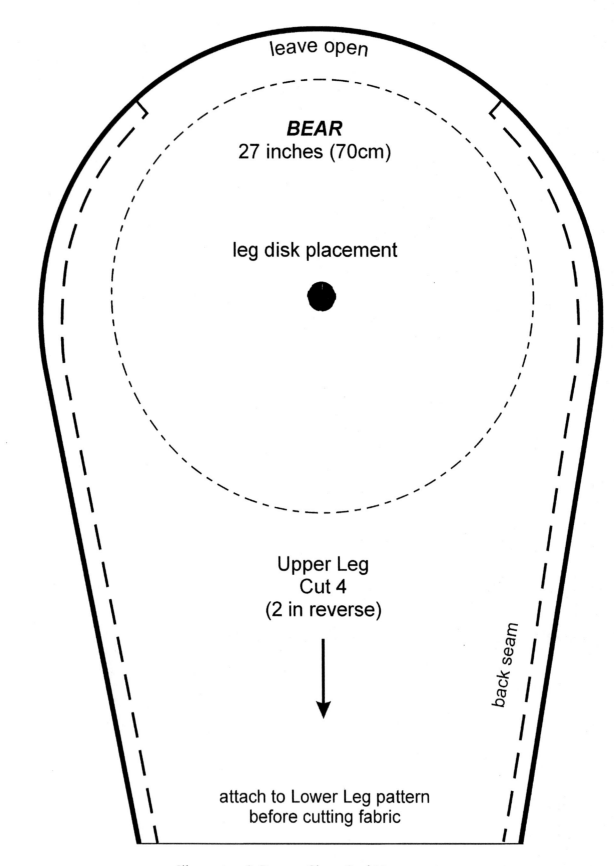
Illustration 8. Pattern Sheet 2 of 11

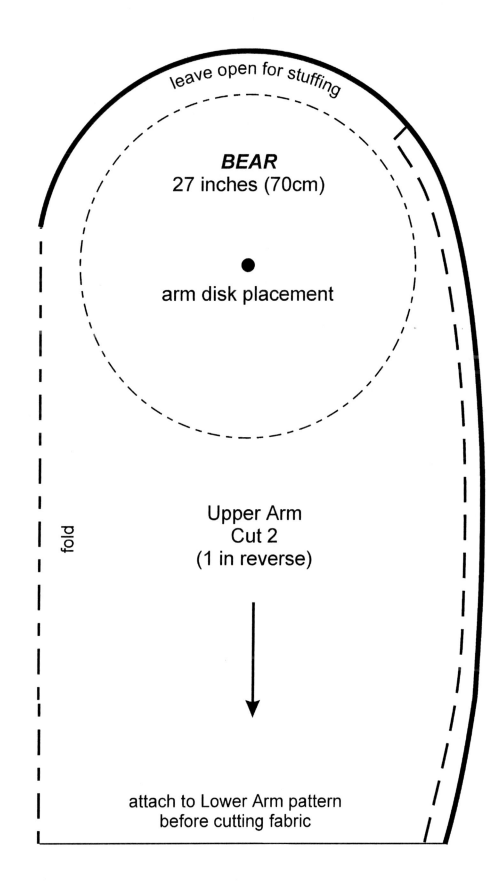

Illustration 9. Pattern Sheet 3 of 11

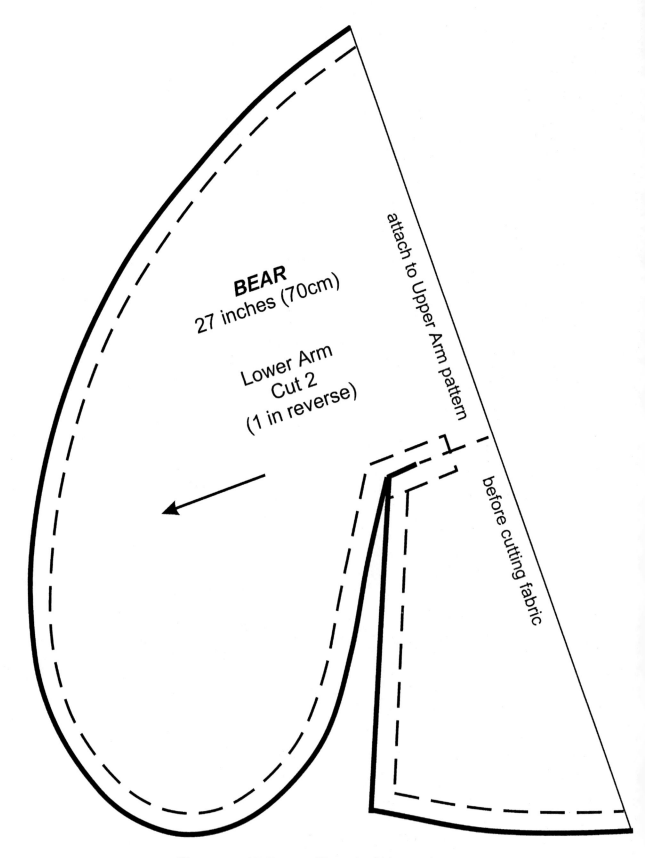

Illustration 10. Pattern Sheet 4 of 11

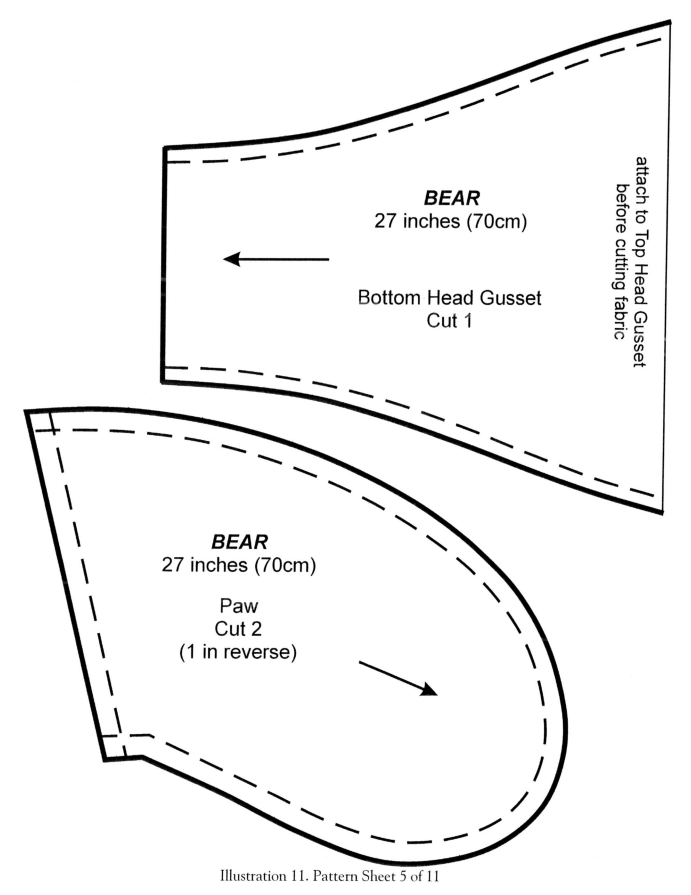

Illustration 11. Pattern Sheet 5 of 11

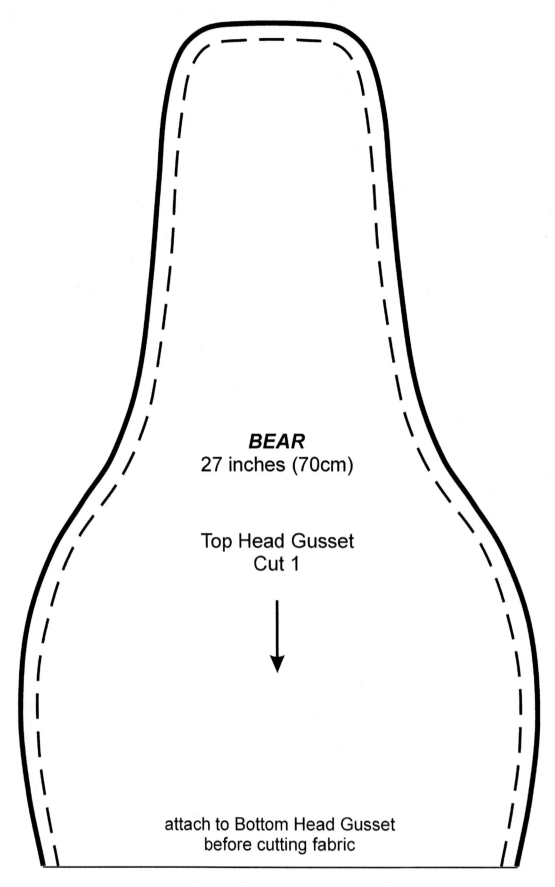

Illustration 12. Pattern Sheet 6 of 11

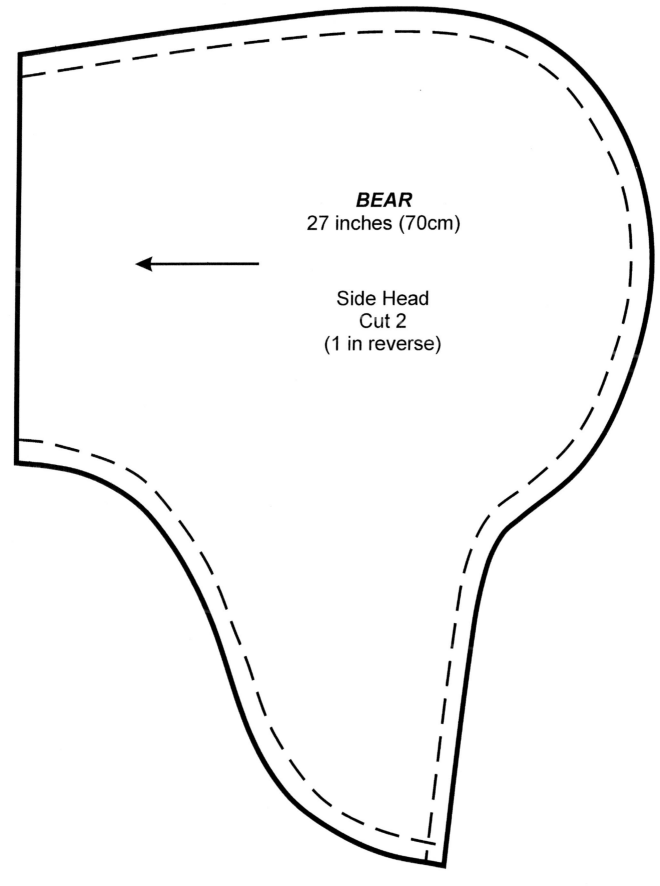

Illustration 13. Pattern Sheet 7 of 11

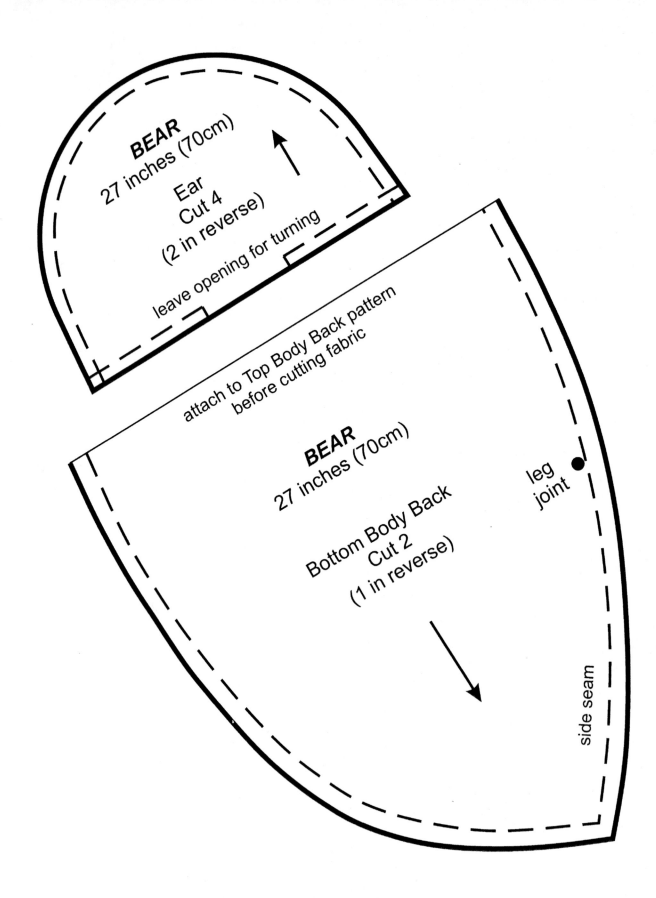

Illustration 14. Pattern Sheet 8 of 11

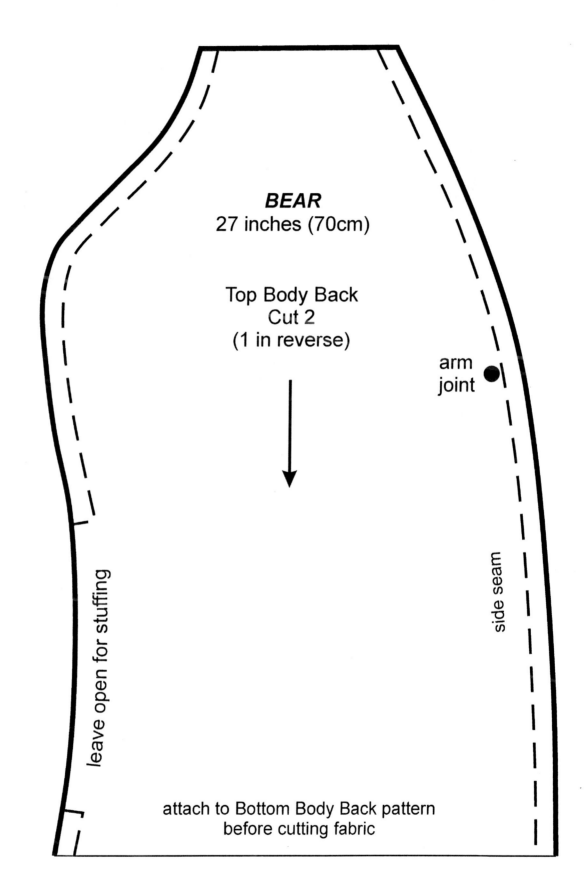

Illustration 15. Pattern Sheet 9 of 11

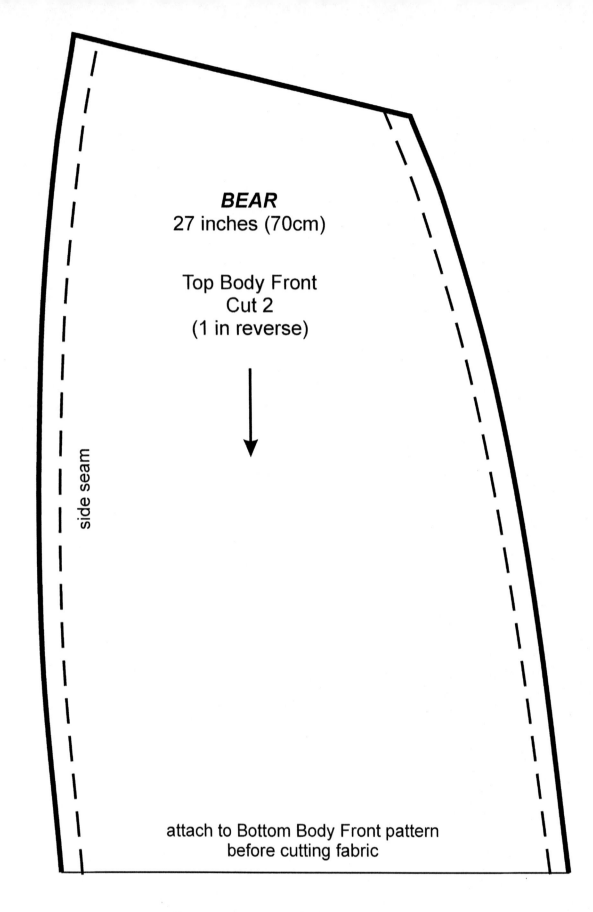

Illustration 16. Pattern Sheet 10 of 11

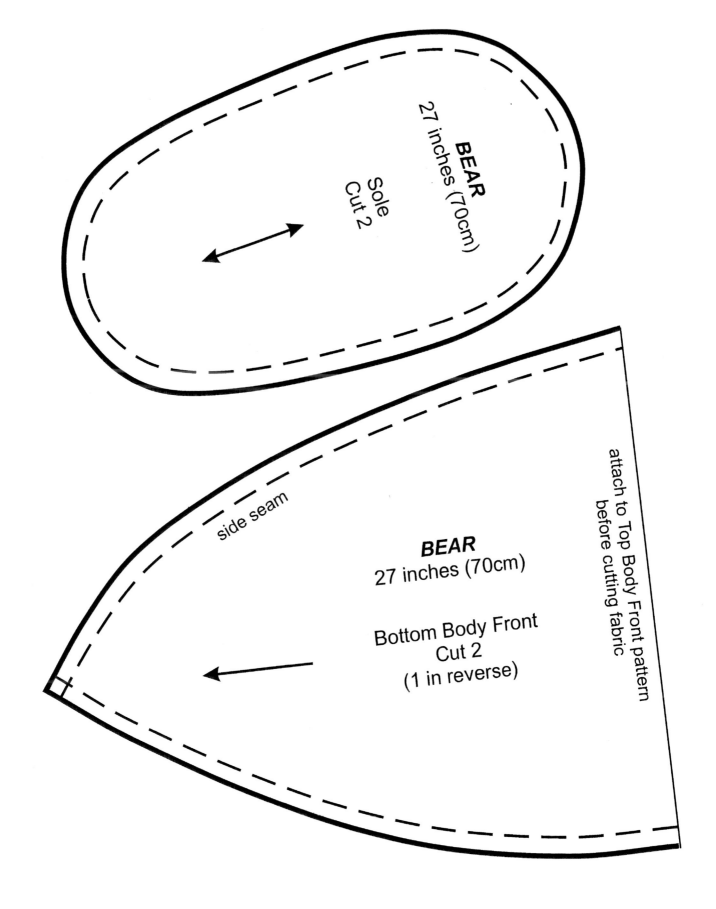

Illustration 17. Pattern Sheet 11 of 11

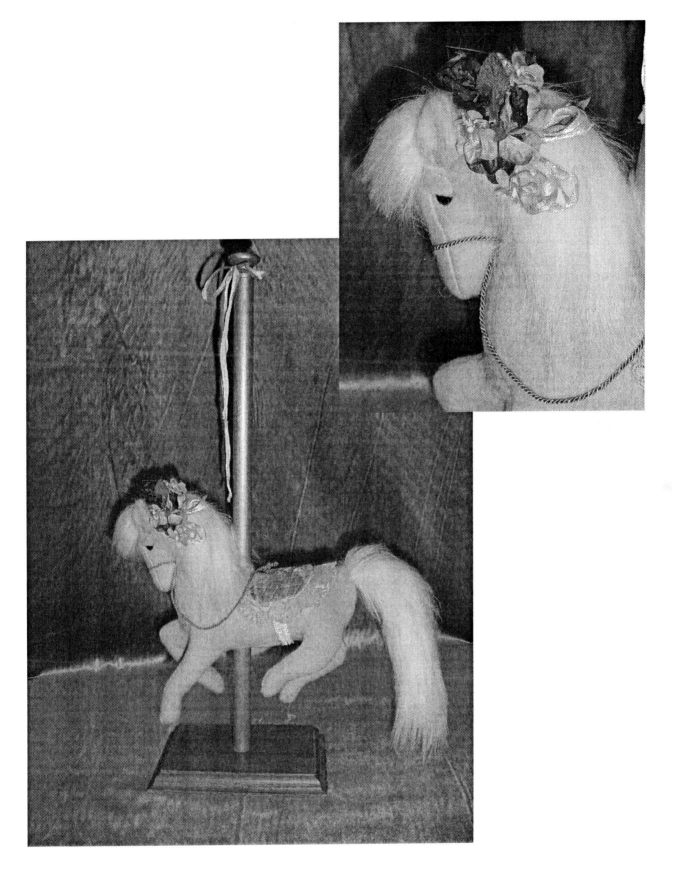

CAROUSEL HORSE
Size: 15 inches (40cm) – Advanced Level

MATERIALS:

1/3 yard (33cm) of 1/8-inch (.31cm) mohair for body
6-inch x 12-inch (15cm x 30cm) piece of upholstery material for saddle
15-inch (40cm) square of recycled fur or 3-inch (8cm) long mohair for mane and tail
Ribbon for pole decoration
1 yard (91cm) of ruffle for saddle
1 yard (91cm) of gold braid for reins
Two 7mm eyes, glass or plastic
One 20-ounce bag of fiberfill
Upholstery thread for attaching eyes and closing seams
Sewing machine thread, color to match fur
One 15-inch (40cm) long wood pole, 3/4-inch (2cm) in diameter
One fancy finial for top of pole
One 10-inch x 6-inch (25cm x 15cm) wood oval plaque for base
Gold paint for pole
Wood stain for base
One bottle tacky glue

This diagram represents all the pieces required to complete the *Carousel Horse*, laid out on the straight of the fabric. More than one piece of fabric may be required for laying out the pattern pieces.

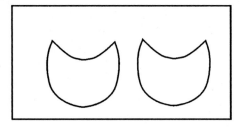

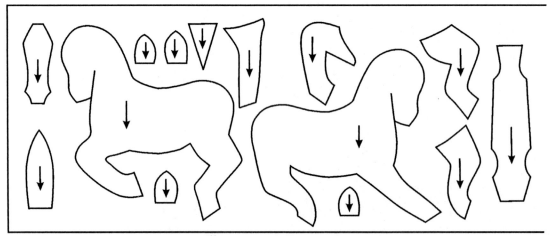

Illustration 1. Pattern Layout

INSTRUCTIONS:

Sew the head together along the neck from the nose to the top of the neck.

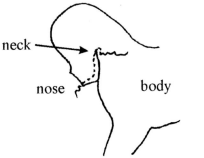

Illustration 2. Sew the Head

Sew the body gussets together. Sew the leg pieces to the gusset.

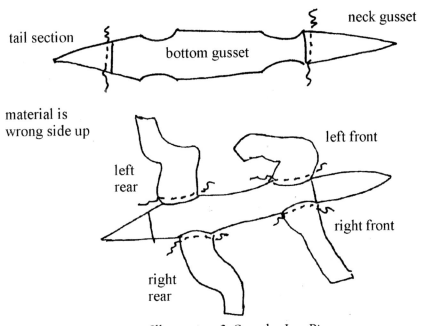

Illustration 3. Sew the Leg Pieces

Pin the left side of the body to the left side of the gusset, matching the legs. Sew from the neck to the back of the body. Repeat for the right side.

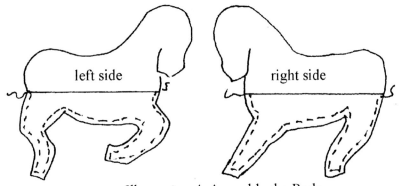

Illustration 4. Assemble the Body

Sew the nose gusset on the front of the head. Sew both sides, from the nose to the top of the head.

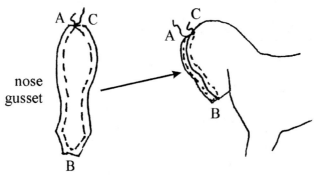

Illustration 5. Sew the Nose

Sew from the back of the head to the opening for stuffing, and from the other side of the opening to the tail section.

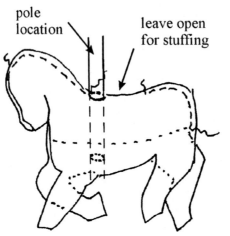

Illustration 6. Sew the Back Seam

Sew the inner and outer ears together. Ease the outer ear to the inner ear.

Illustration 7. Sew the Ears

Make armatures for the neck and legs. Follow the patterns for the bends in the leg armatures. Bend the ends of the wire into tight loops for safety. Loop the end of the neck armature around the front leg armature.

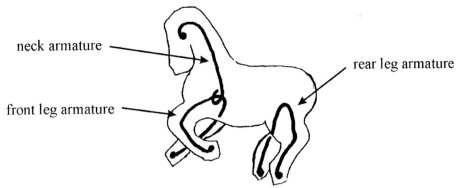

Illustration 8. Make the Armatures

Turn the body. Insert the armatures in the legs and stuff the legs. Stuff the head around the neck armature. Stuff the remainder of the body and close.

Cut the mane and tail to fit. The mane is 7 inches x 4 inches (17cm x 10cm). Sew the mane to the body from the top of the head to the back opening. The tail is 7 inches x 3 inches (17cm x 7cm). Fold the tail in half and sew together. Attach the tail to the body.

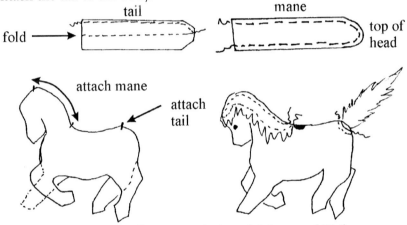

Illustration 9. Attach Mane and Tail

Make the base. Drill a hole in the base to match the diameter of the pole. Stain the base with wax shoe polish. Attach the finial to the pole. Sand the pole and paint gold. Insert the pole through the horse from the base of the neck to the bottom gusset. Adjust the horse to the position desired and mark where the pole enters the body. Slide the horse up the pole and coat the pole between the marks with glue. Slide the horse back down to the marks and set aside to dry.

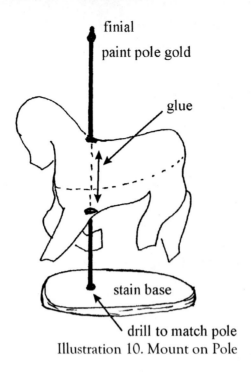

Illustration 10. Mount on Pole

Glue the ears in place. Make a hole in the head, put fabric glue in the hole and insert the ears about 1/4 inch (1cm). Attach both eyes and pull the thread tight to set in the eyes.

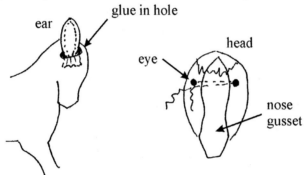

Illustration 11. Attach Ears and Eyes

Sew the trim to the saddle top. Sew the saddle top and bottom together. Turn and stuff lightly. Quilt the saddle. Attach the saddle to the horse with a braided cord cinch.

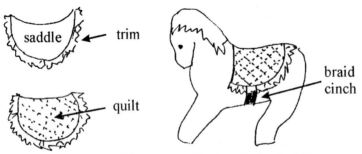

Illustration 12. Attach the Saddle

Make the bridle from braided cord. Loop the braid around the muzzle and glue together under the muzzle. Make the reins to loop over the neck. Attach the reins to the bridle. Tie ribbon around the top of the pole for decoration.

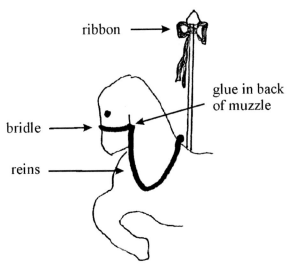

Illustration 13. Attach the Reins

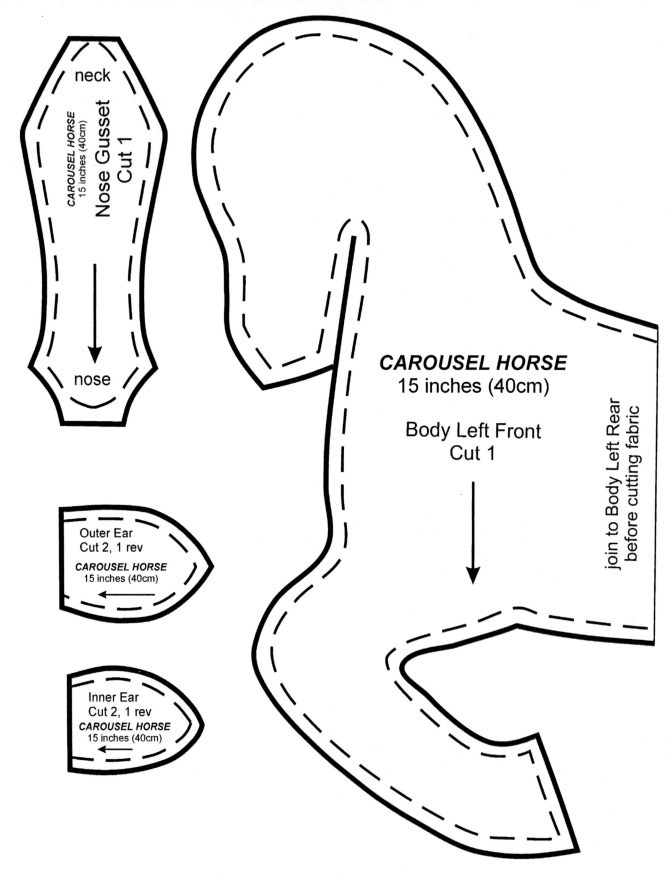

Illustration 14. Pattern Sheet 1 of 5

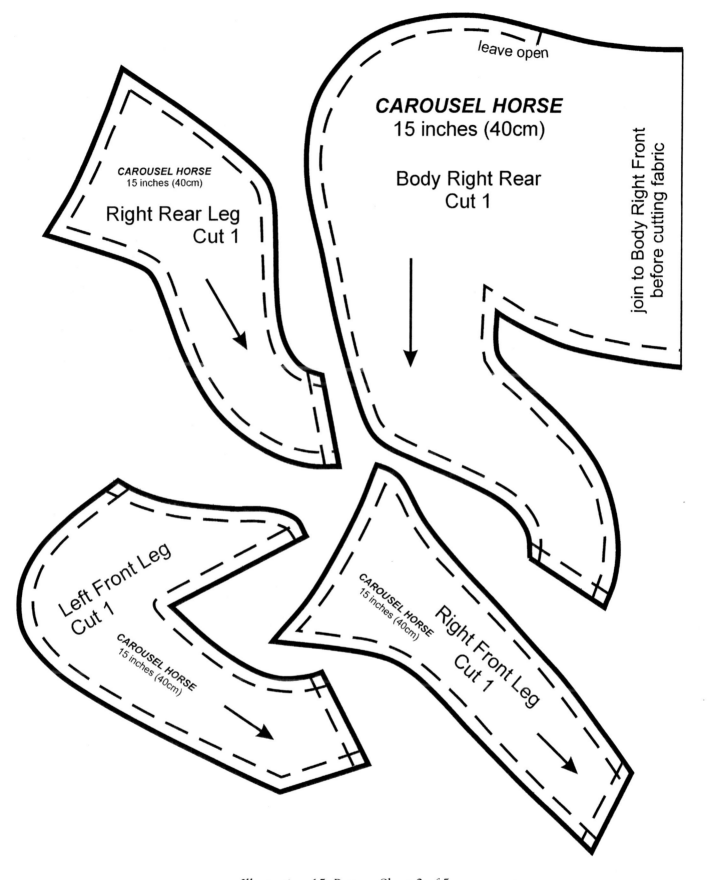

Illustration 15. Pattern Sheet 2 of 5

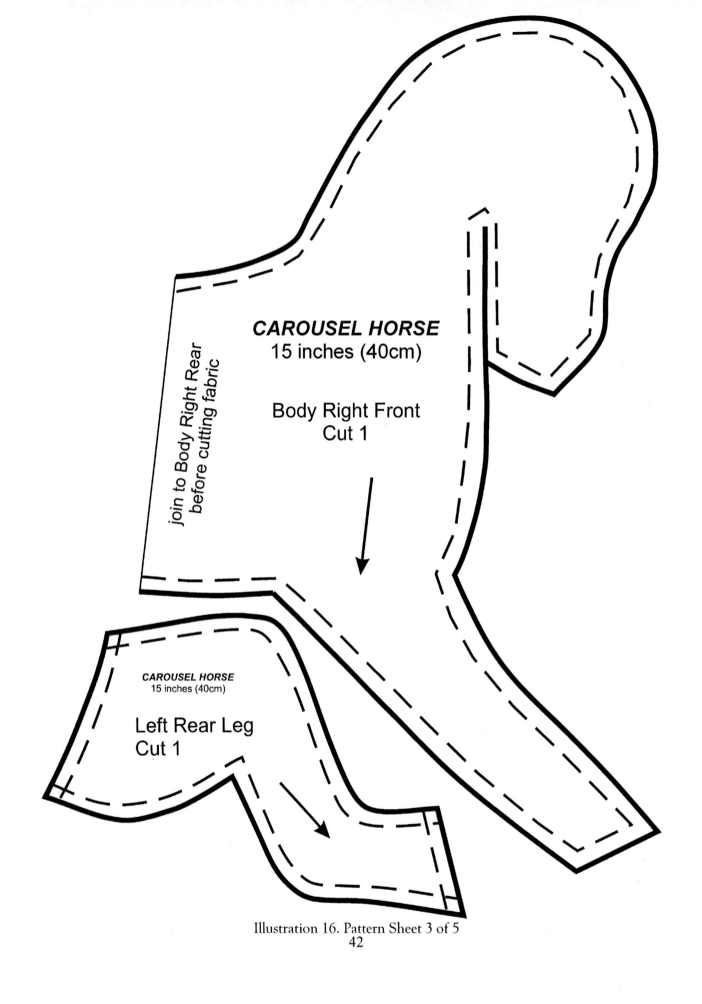

Illustration 16. Pattern Sheet 3 of 5

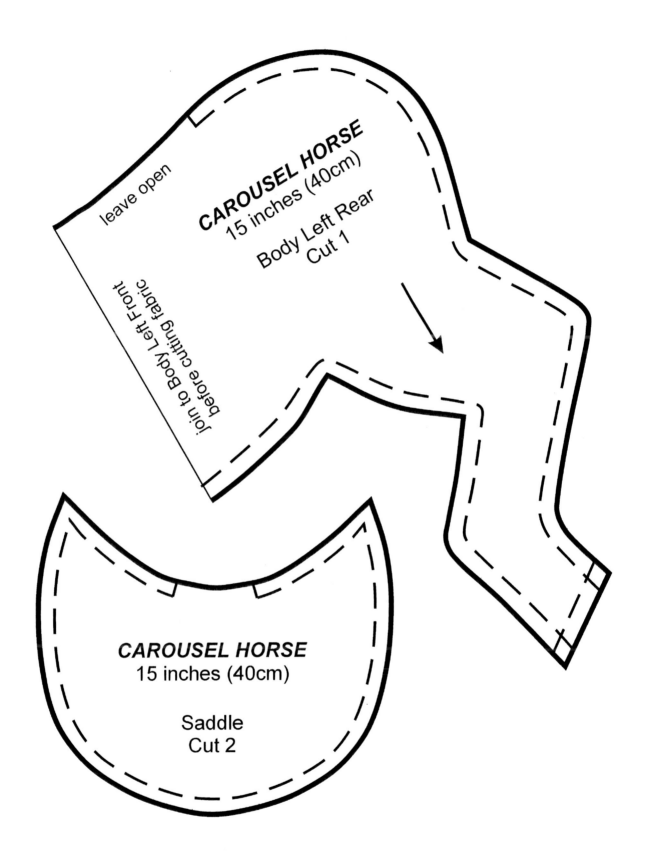

Illustration 17. Pattern Sheet 4 of 5

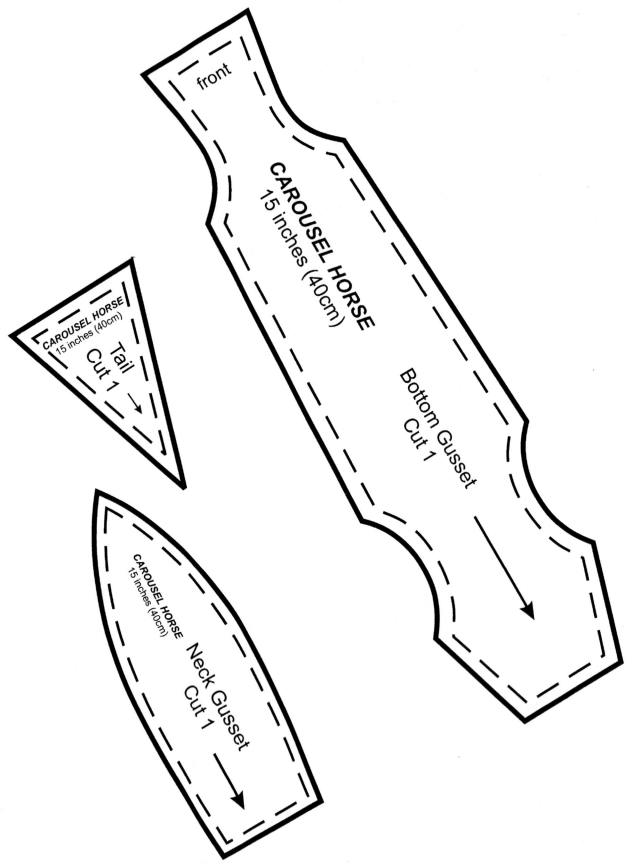

Illustration 18. Pattern Sheet 5 of 5

CAT
Size: 18 inches (45cm) – Advanced Level

MATERIALS:

1 yard (91cm) of mohair, color of body
12 inch (30cm) square of long 3 inch (8cm) white fur for face and tip of tail
12 inch (30cm) square of 100 percent wool felt for paw pads
Two 8mm eyes, glass or plastic
Ten 2 inch (5cm) diameter fiber disks for head, arm and leg joints
Two 3 1/2 inch (9cm) diameter fiber disks for face joint
Six 1 1/2 inch (4cm) cotter pins or hex head bolts with lock nuts
Eighteen 1/2 inch (1cm) fender washers for joints
One 20 ounce bag of fiberfill
One bag of plastic pellets (for weight)
Pink Perlé cotton thread for embroidering nose
Black Perlé cotton thread for outlining nose and mouth
Upholstery thread for whiskers, attaching eyes and closing seams
Sewing machine thread, color to match fur
Ribbon for bow

This diagram represents all the pieces required to complete the *Cat*, laid out on the straight of the fabric. More than one piece of fabric may be required for laying out the pattern pieces.

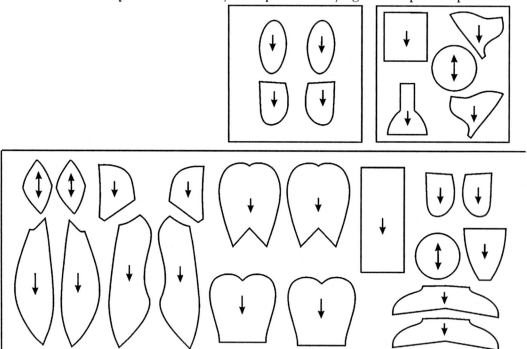

Illustration 1. Pattern Layout

INSTRUCTIONS:

Sew the two side face pieces to the center face gusset. Pin the gusset to the side head before sewing, to keep the pieces from moving. Sew the two side face pieces together from the nose down to the neck edge. Sew the long fur face disk, leaving the bottom open for turning and stuffing. The seam diameter should match the diameter of the cardboard face joint disk.

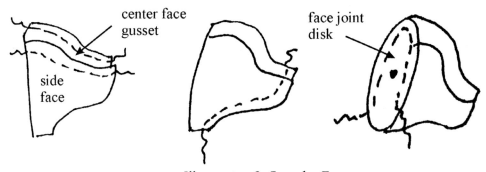

Illustration 2. Sew the Face

Sew the two side head pieces to the back head gusset. Sew the short fur face disk.

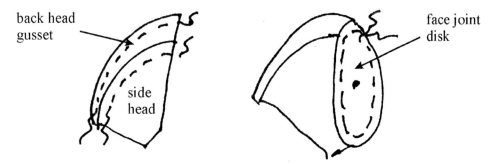

Illustration 3. Sew the Head

Fold the ears and sew. Make a slit along the fold to turn.

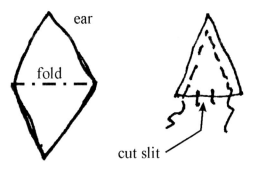

Illustration 4. Sew the Ears

Sew the front seam of the body fronts together. Sew the back seam of the body backs together, leaving an opening for stuffing. Sew the front to the back along the side seams. Leave the neck open.

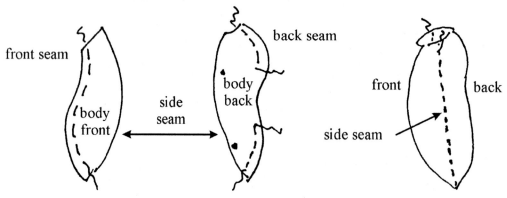

Illustration 5. Body Seams

Sew the paws and paw pads to the arms. Make sure to end up with a right and left arm, not two identical arms! Sew the arms together, leaving the top open for stuffing.

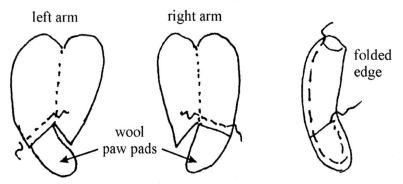

Illustration 6. Sew the Paws and Arms

Sew the feet to the legs. Sew the legs together, leaving the top open for stuffing. Sew the soles to the legs.

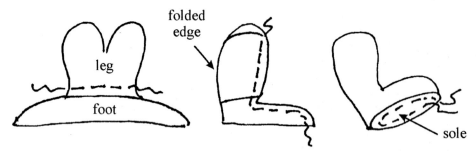

Illustration 7. Sew the Legs and Soles

Sew the tip of the tail to the tail. Fold the tail and sew, leaving an opening to turn.

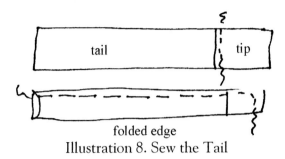

Illustration 8. Sew the Tail

Make disks for the arms (four) legs (four), head (two) and face (two). Refer to the **Basic Directions** and list of materials for sizes.

Make a hole in the center of the fabric face disks in both the face and head pieces. Attach the face to the head with a cotter pin joint. Stuff both pieces. Insert the head joint cotter pin, fender washer and cardboard disk. Close the neck around the disk.

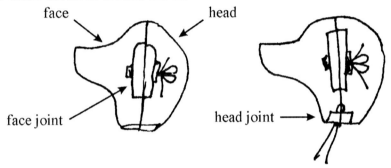

Illustration 9. Head Joints

Cut the fur off the muzzle section. Trim with scissors as close to the backing as possible. Attach the eyes to the head in the trimmed area, close to the edge of the long fur. Attach the ears and embroider the nose and mouth.

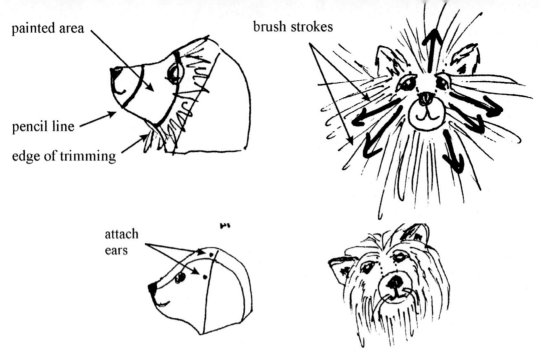

Illustration 10. Finish the Head

Join the head to the body, then the arms and finally the legs. Stuff the arms, legs and finally the body. Close all seams – the body seam last in case a little more stuffing is required.

With a pencil, mark the muzzle to show the painted area. Brush out the fur all around the muzzle. Paint the muzzle. Paint the fur, using outward strokes, around the entire face.
Illustration 11. Paint the Face

Let the paint dry completely. Use a small stiff wire brush to brush the painted area and the fur around the face to soften and remove excess paint.

Sew a length of upholstery thread through the muzzle to form a whisker on both sides. Tie an overhand knot near the muzzle and insert a needle through the knot to guide the knot up tight to the face. Remove the needle and pull the knot tight from both ends of the whisker. Repeat for the other side.

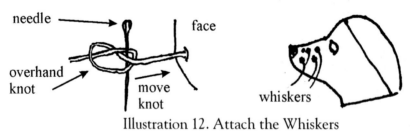

Illustration 12. Attach the Whiskers

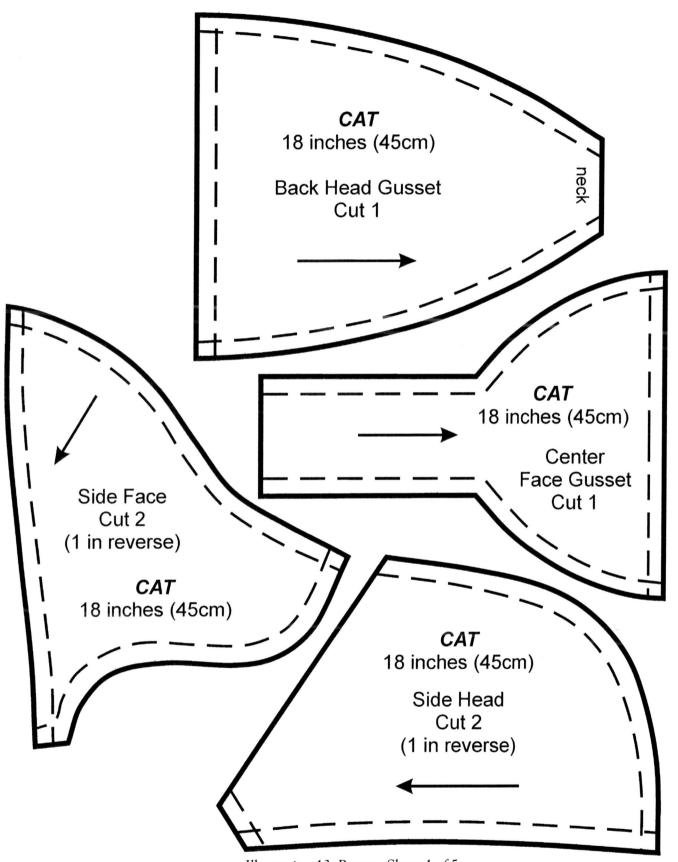

Illustration 13. Pattern Sheet 1 of 5

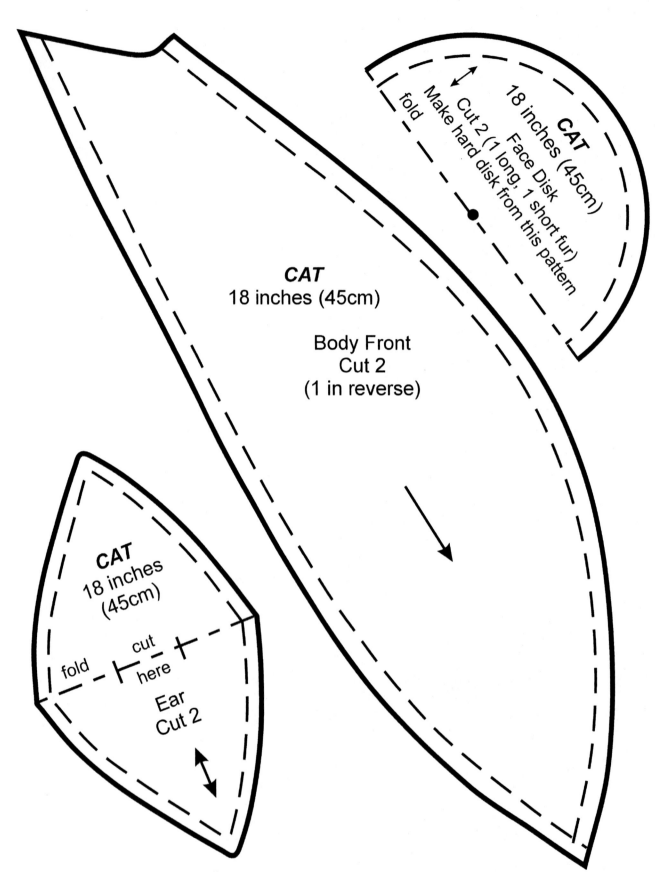

Illustration 14. Pattern Sheet 2 of 5

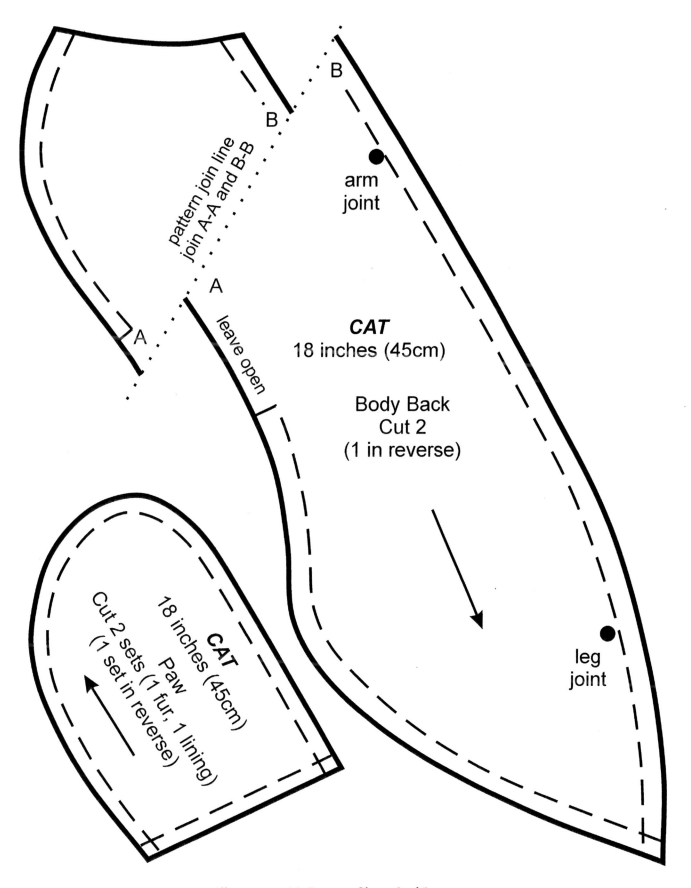

Illustration 15. Pattern Sheet 3 of 5

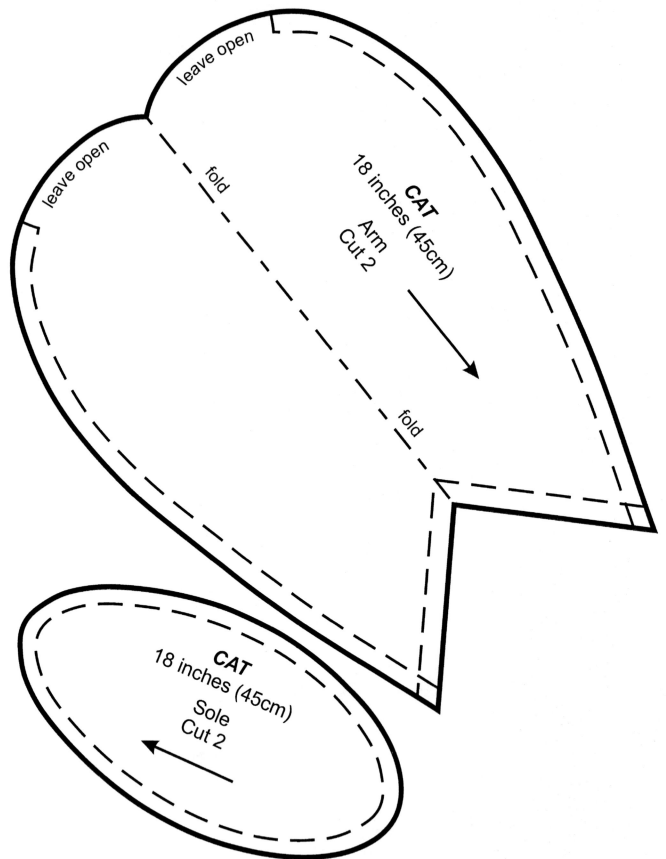

Illustration 16. Pattern Sheet 4 of 5

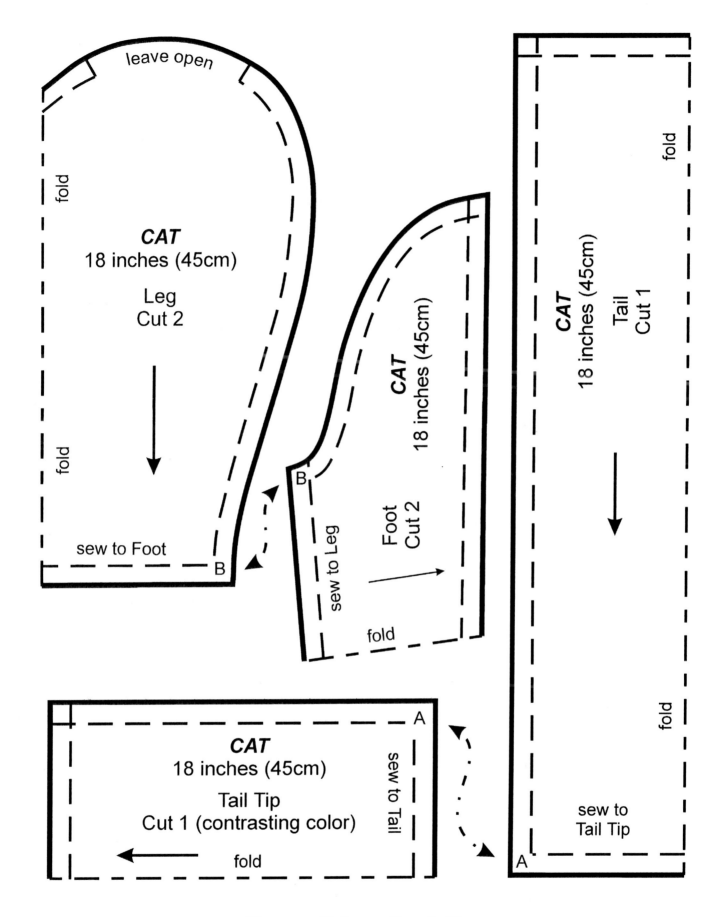

Illustration 17. Pattern Sheet 5 of 5

DOG
Size: 8 inches (20cm) – Intermediate Level

MATERIALS:

1/4 yard (25cm) of string mohair, white
6 inch (15cm) square of upholstery material for paws
8 inch (20cm) square of 2 inch (5cm) white fur for ears
Two 7mm eyes, glass or plastic
Two 1 1/2 inch (4cm) diameter fiber disks for head joint
One 1 1/2 inch (4cm) cotter pin
Four 1/2 inch (1cm) fender washer for joint
One 16 ounce bag of fiberfill
Black Perlé cotton thread for embroidering nose and mouth
Upholstery thread for attaching eyes and closing seams
Sewing machine thread, color to match fur
Firm, bendable wire (#16 gauge) for leg armatures
Black and brown (burnt umber) dye pens to highlight beard and ears

This diagram represents all the pieces required to complete the *Dog*, laid out on the straight of the fabric. More than one piece of fabric may be required for laying out the pattern pieces.

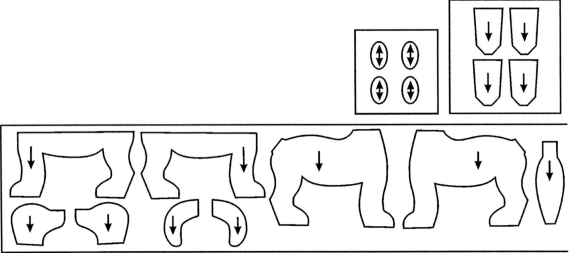

Illustration 1. Pattern Layout

INSTRUCTIONS:

Sew the center head gusset to the side head pieces. Pin the gusset to the side head before sewing to keep the pieces from moving. Sew the two side head pieces together from the nose down to the neck edge.

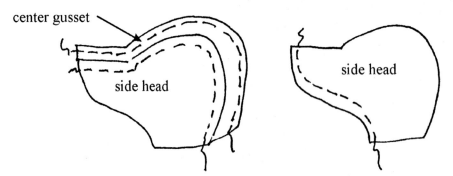

Illustration 2. Sew the Head

Sew the front and back of the ears together. Leave the bottom open for turning.

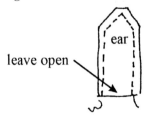

Illustration 3. Sew the Ears

Sew the underbody together, leaving an opening in the center.

Illustration 4. Sew Underbody

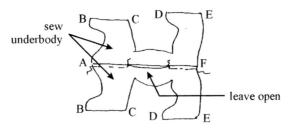

Sew each side of the body to the underbody from A to B, C to D and E to F. Sew the two side body pieces together from A to the neck, from F to the tail and from the tail to the neck.

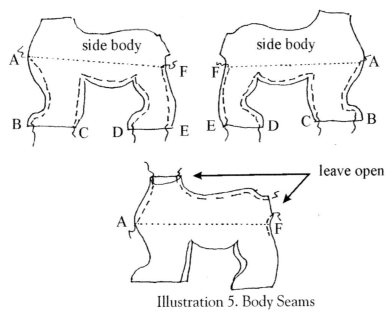

Illustration 5. Body Seams

Sew the soles to the legs. Sew the two pieces of the tail together, leaving the bottom open for turning.

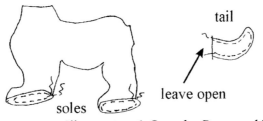

Illustration 6. Sew the Paws and Tail

Turn all pieces right side out. Stuff the head and insert the top part of the cotter pin joint before closing the neck around the fiber disk. Trim the fur around the muzzle, leaving a beard. Use a black dye pen to shade the area around the eyes and behind the beard. Attach the eyes and embroider the nose and mouth.

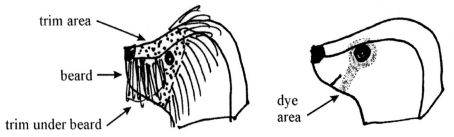

Illustration 7. Finish the Head

Before stuffing the body, make two wire armatures to strengthen the legs. Make one armature for the front legs and one for the rear legs. Make loops for the feet and bend so the legs stand upright.

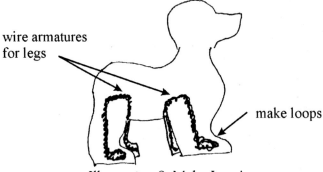

Illustration 8. Make Leg Armatures

Attach the head to the body with the cotter pin joint. Insert the armatures in the legs and stuff the body. Stuff the tail lightly and join to the body.

Illustration 9. Assembly

Do not stuff the ears. Attach the ears to the head with a ladder stitch.

Illustration 10. Attach the Ears

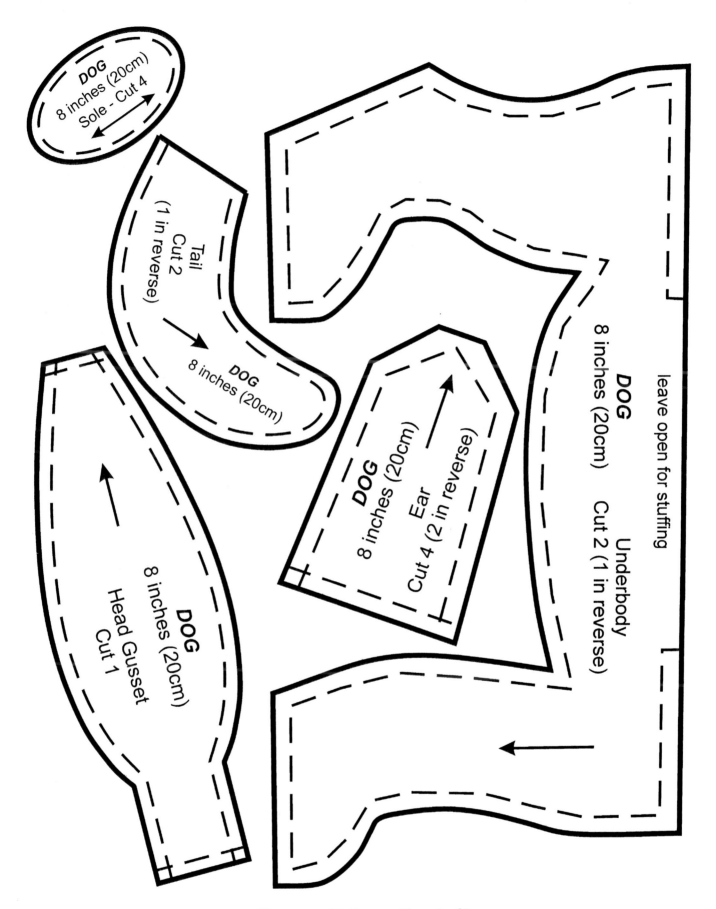

Illustration 11. Pattern Sheet 1 of 2

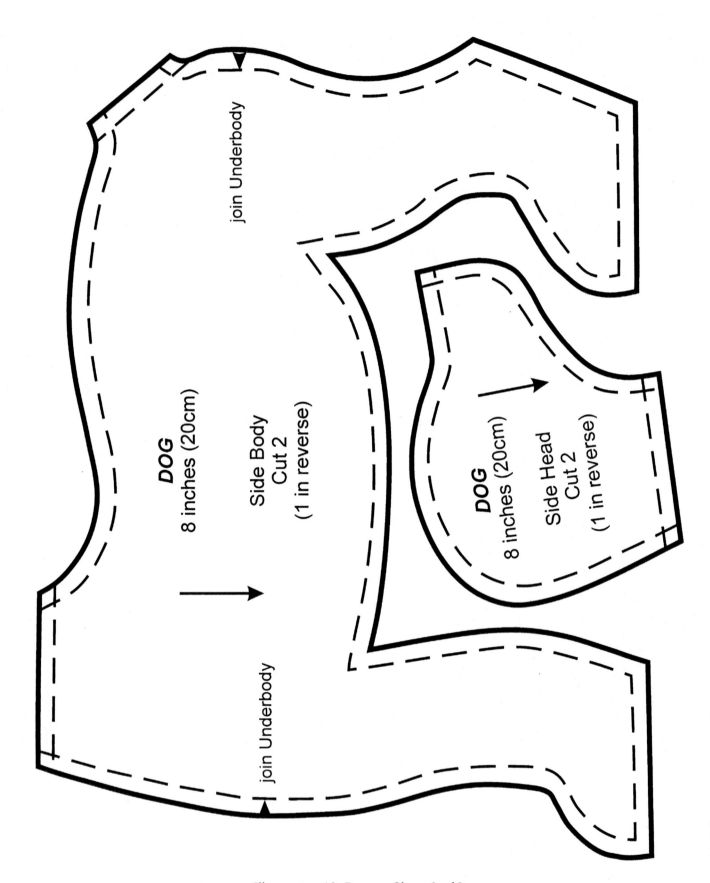

Illustration 12. Pattern Sheet 2 of 2

ELEPHANT
Size: 8 inches (20cm) – Beginning Level

MATERIALS:

1/4 yard (25cm) of 1/8 inch (.31cm) gray mohair or wool felt
5 inch (10cm) square of white wool felt for tusks
Two 6mm eyes, glass or plastic
Ten 3/4 inch (2cm) balloon disks for joints (find at party supply shop)
Five 1 1/2 inch (4cm) cotter pins
Fifteen 1/2 inch (2cm) fender washers
One 16 ounce bag of fiberfill
Nylon thread for attaching eyes and closing seams
Sewing machine thread, color to match fur
Fine point fabric dye marker, black

This diagram represents all the pieces required to complete the *Elephant*, laid out on the straight of the fabric. More than one piece of fabric may be required for laying out the pattern pieces.

Illustration 1. Pattern Layout

INSTRUCTIONS:

Sew the two head pieces together, leaving the neck open. Sew the ears together, leaving an opening for turning. Hand sew the tusks, right side out, stitching close to the edge (the tusks are too small to turn).

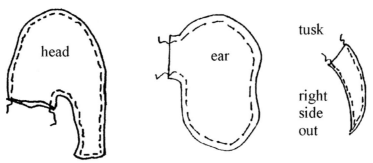

Illustration 2. Sew the Head Pieces

Sew the two body backs together, leaving an opening in the center back for stuffing. Sew the dart on the front. Pin the front and back together, to keep the pieces from moving. Sew the front to the back, leaving the neck open.

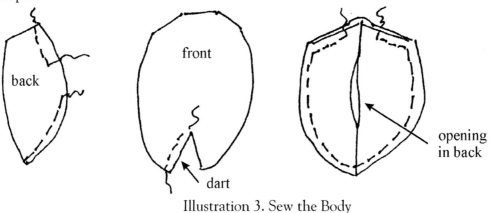

Illustration 3. Sew the Body

Sew the arm pieces together, leaving an opening at the top for stuffing. Sew the paw pads to the arms. Sew the legs the same as the arms.

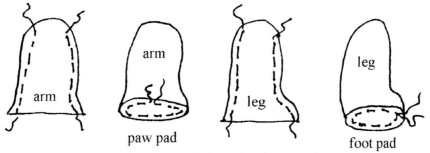

Illustration 4. Sew the Arms and Legs

Turn the head, ears, body, arms and legs. Make up the part of the joint inside the head (washer on cotter pin, fender washer and balloon disk). Stuff and close the head around the disk. Attach the eyes. Use the fabric marker to darken the area around the eyes. Attach the tusks and ears (no stuffing required).

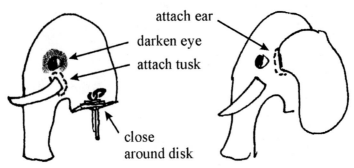

Illustration 5. Complete the Head

Gather and close the body at the neck. Join the head to the body. Join the arms and legs. Stuff the arms, legs and body. Close the seams.

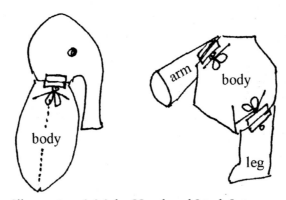

Illustration 6. Make Head and Limb Joints

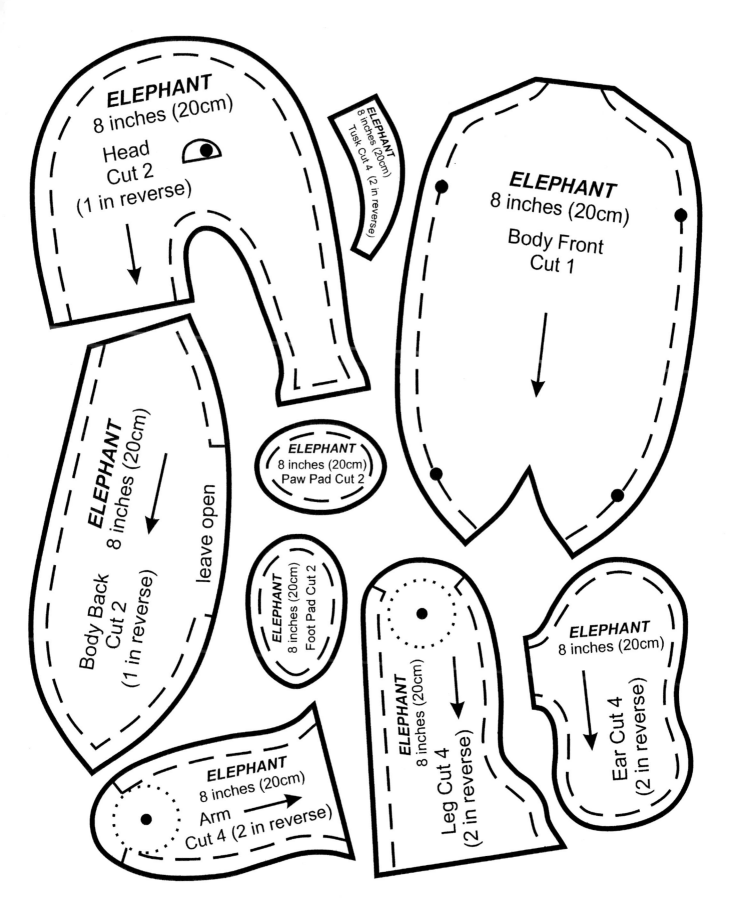

Illustration 7. Pattern Sheet 1 of 1

GIRAFFE
Size: 10 inches (25cm) – Intermediate Level

MATERIALS:

1/3 yard (33cm) of mohair, light gold
4 inch (20cm) square upholstery material for horns
4 inch (10cm) square upholstery material for soles
5 inch x 3/4 inch (12cm x 2cm) of 1/4 inch straight mohair for mane
Two 6mm eyes, glass or plastic
One 16 ounce bag fiberfill
One skein brown Perlé cotton thread for tail
Upholstery thread for attaching eyes and closing seams
Sewing machine thread, color to match fur
Fabric paint marker for spots, brown, fine point and bold point
24 inch (30cm) length of stiff bendable wire for leg armatures

This diagram represents all the pieces required to complete the *Giraffe*, laid out on the straight of the fabric. More than one piece of fabric may be required for laying out the pattern pieces.

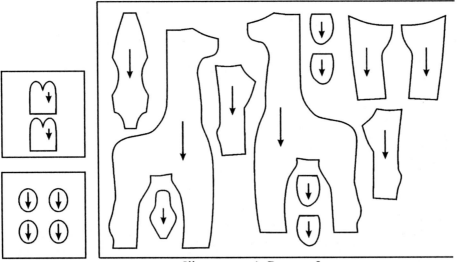

Illustration 1. Pattern Layout

INSTRUCTIONS:

Sew the face to both body sides. Sew from the nose down the neck. Fold the mane, fur side out, and sew to the inside of one side of the body. Position the other side of the body over the mane and sew through the mane down the neck and back.

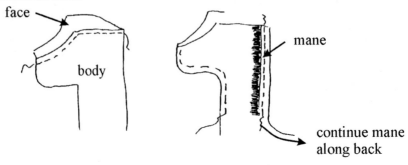

Illustration 2. Sew the Head and Neck

Sew the inside legs to the bottom gusset. Sew the bottom gusset to the body at the legs. Sew the soles onto the legs.

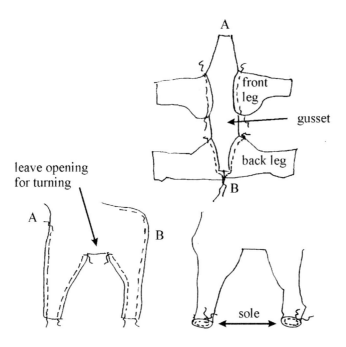

Illustration 3. Complete the Body

Sew the ears together. Fold the horn and sew.

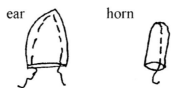

Illustration 4. Sew the Ears and Horns

Make leg and neck armatures from three pieces of wire. The leg armatures are "U" shaped – one for the back legs and the other for the front legs. Loop the neck armature around the front leg armature. Bend each end of the armatures into tight loops so there are no sharp ends.   Illustration 5. Armatures

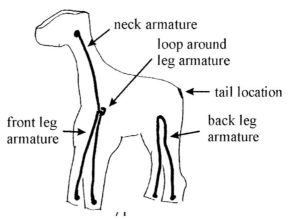

Turn the *Giraffe* right side out. Insert the armatures and stuff. Close the seams. Turn the horns and the ears. Lightly stuff the horns. Attach the horns and ears to the head.

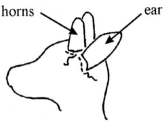

Illustration 6. Attach Horns and Ears

Wind the brown cotton thread into twelve 6 inch (15cm) loops. Cut through the loops once, leaving twelve 12 inch (30cm) strands of thread. Attach the center of the group of strands to the body at the tail location. Divide the strands into three groups of eight strands each. Braid the tail about 1 1/4 inches (3cm) and knot. Cut the tail about 1/2 inch (1cm) past the knot. Comb out the tail.

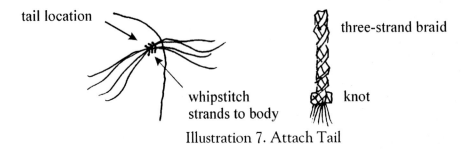

Illustration 7. Attach Tail

Shave the muzzle. Use the fine point fabric paint marker to paint the nose, mouth, eyebrows, forehead, inner ears and horn tips. Use the broad point marker to make the *Giraffe's* spots. The underbody and the legs below the knees do not have spots. Outline the feet to make hoofs.

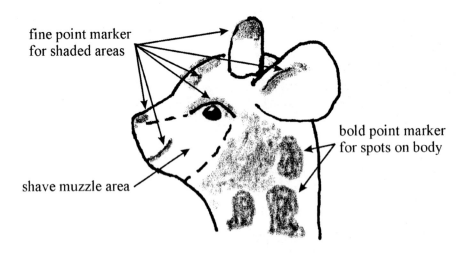

Illustration 8. Paint the Head

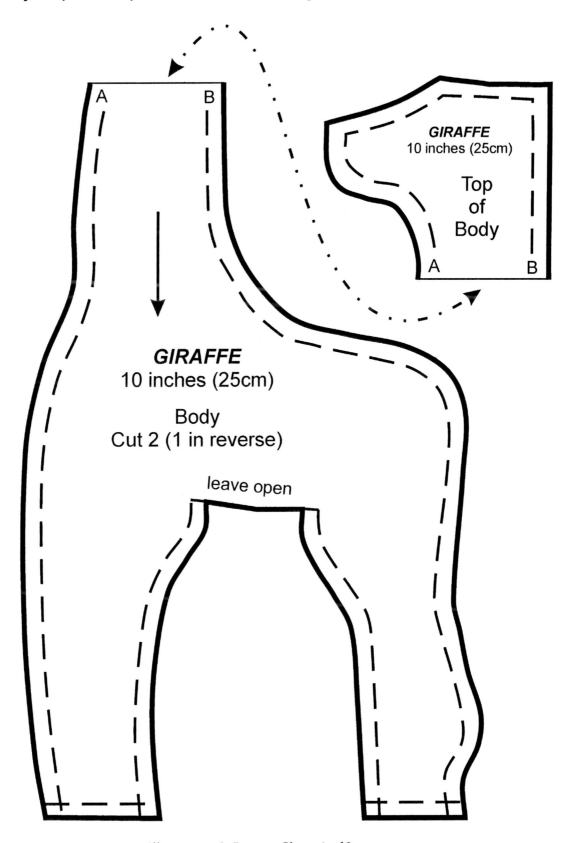

Illustration 9. Pattern Sheet 1 of 2

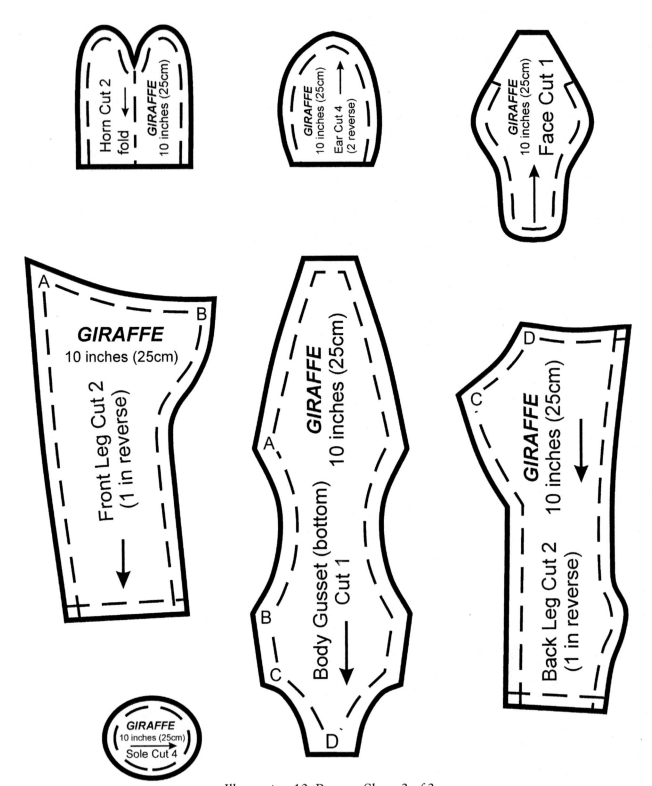

Illustration 10. Pattern Sheet 2 of 2

HARE EXTRAORDINAIRE
Size: 13inches (33cm) – Intermediate Level

MATERIALS:

1/4 yard (25cm) of beige coat wool (purchase at second hand store) or 1/2 inch (1cm) mohair
6 inch x 9 inch (15cm x 23cm) piece of beige suede material for ears
18 inch (45 cm) square of maroon wool felt for coat
9 inch x 10 inch (23cm x 25cm) piece of white wool felt for collar
7 inch x 5 inch (18cm x 13cm) piece of gold wool felt for vest
1 inch x 18 inch (3cm x 46cm) piece of black wool felt for bow tie
2 inch (5cm) square of thin leather for eyebrows
Four 2 inch (5cm) diameter fiber disks for leg joints
Six 1 1/2 inch (4cm) diameter fiber disks for arm and neck joints
Five 2 inch (5cm) cotter pins for joints
Fifteen 3/8 inch (.9cm) fender washers for joints
Six gold beads for buttons on vest
Fabric glue
Two 8mm glass eyes
36 inches (91cm) of wire for ears (#16 gauge, bendable but firm enough to hold shape)
One 20 ounce bag of polyester fiberfill
Nylon thread for attaching eyes and closing seams
Upholstery thread for attaching ears
Fabric or acrylic paint, 2 ounce bottles in white, brown and black
Stiff bristle brush – narrow and wide
Sewing machine thread to match fabric

This diagram represents all the pieces required to complete *Hare Extraordinaire*, laid out on the straight of the fabric. More than one piece of fabric may be required for laying out the pattern pieces.

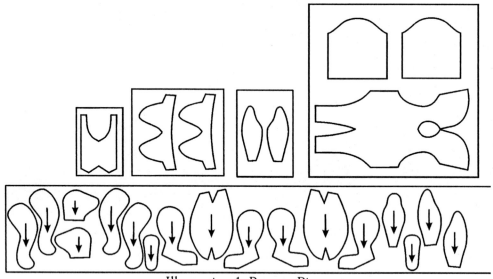

Illustration 1. Pattern Pieces

Sew the two side head pieces together, stitching from the neck to the nose. Insert the head gusset between the side head pieces and stitch from the nose over the top of the head to the neck.

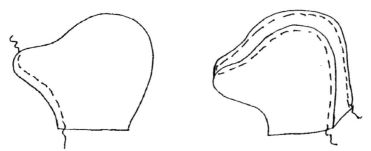

Illustration 2. Sew the Head

Sew two ears together, each with outside and inside (lining). Bend the wire to the shape of the ear, using the seam as a guide. Make small loops in both ends of the wire for attaching the ears. Turn the ear right side out and insert the wire form. Stitch along the inside of the wire to lock in place.

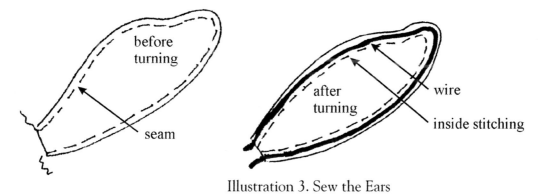

Illustration 3. Sew the Ears

Sew the arm and leg pieces together to form two arms and two legs. Leave the top open for stuffing. Attach the soles to the bottom of the legs.

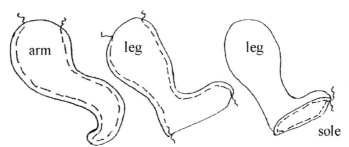

Illustration 4. Sew the Arms and Legs

Sew the darts in the body, and then sew the two body halves together. Leave the top of the body open for stuffing.

Illustration 5. Sew the Body

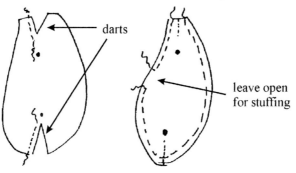

Tape the three parts of the jacket pattern together. Make a cardboard pattern, and then cut the jacket out of a single piece of fabric. Sew two rows of gathering stitches at the top of the sleeves. Gather the sleeves to fit the sleeve opening on the jacket.

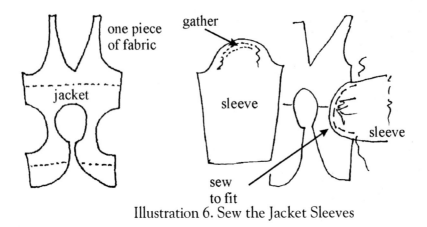

Illustration 6. Sew the Jacket Sleeves

Fold the jacket at the shoulder and sew the jacket side seam and the sleeve seams together. Sew both pieces of the collar together, or use fabric glue, to make a double thick collar. Do not attach the collar to the jacket. The

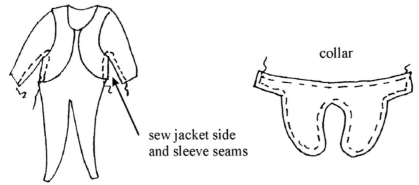

collar is stitched on the *Hare* in the final assembly.

Illustration 7. Finish the Coat and Collar

Refer to the **Basic Instructions** for finishing the head, jointing, stuffing and closing.

The ears are attached after the head is stuffed. Use an awl to open holes in the head for ear placement. Using waxed upholstery thread, start from the bottom of the head and push the needle out through the hole in the head. Loop the thread through the wire loop and push the needle back down through the hole and out the bottom about 1/4 inch (6mm) away. Do the same for the other loop. Insert the ear into the hole and pull the threads tightly. Knot the same as for the eyes. Repeat for the other ear. Stitch the ears to the head where they join.

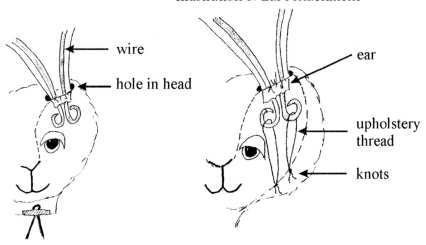

Illustration 8. Ear Attachment

Cut eyebrows from thin leather, shaped to fit. Glue to the head, above the eyes. Paint the face and ears. Refer to the photograph for ideas.

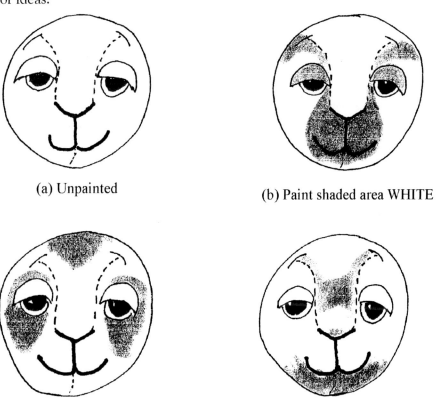

(a) Unpainted

(b) Paint shaded area WHITE

(c) Paint shaded area BLACK

(d) Paint shaded area BROWN

Illustration 9. Paint the Face

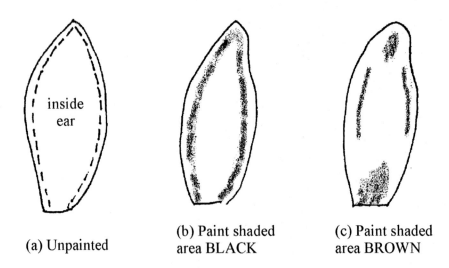

Illustration 10. Paint the Ears

Form the collar around the neck and attach to the shoulders. Sew beads onto the vest. Put the vest on the *Hare* and sew the vest together in back of the neck. Put on the coat and turn the back sleeve cuffs to fit. Tie the bow tie around the neck outside the collar.

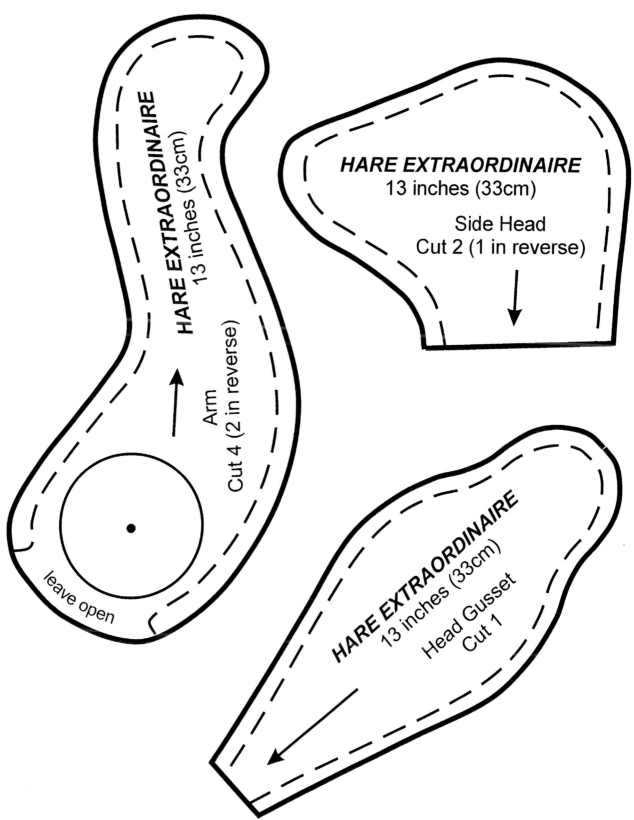

Illustration 11. Pattern Sheet 1 of 7

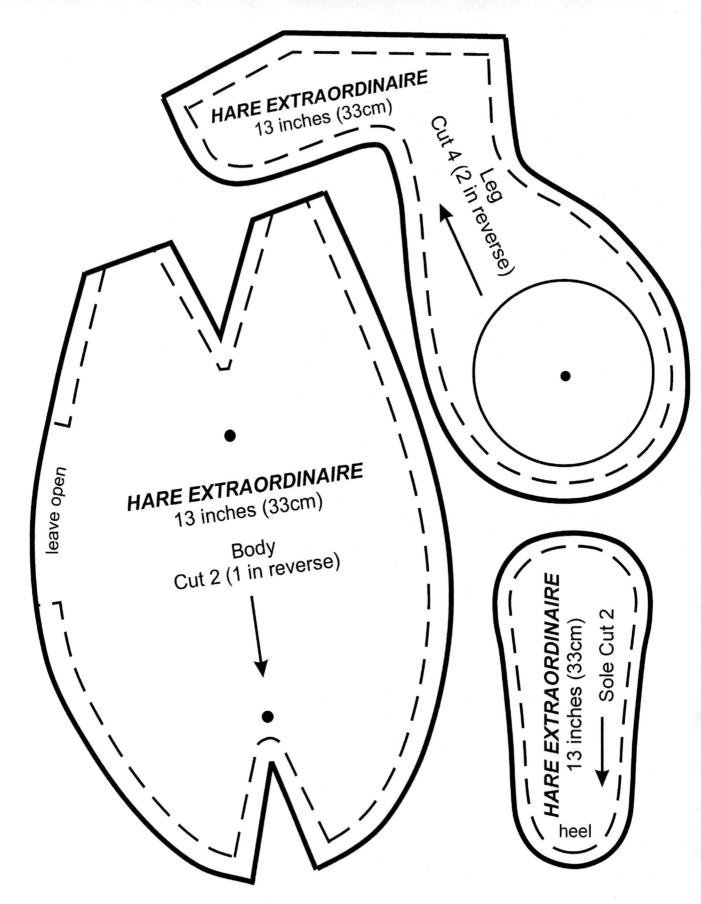

Illustration 12. Pattern Sheet 2 of 7

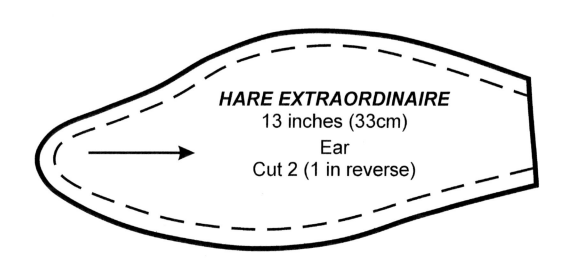

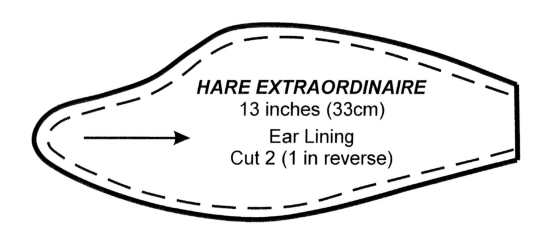

Illustration 13. Pattern Sheet 3 of 7

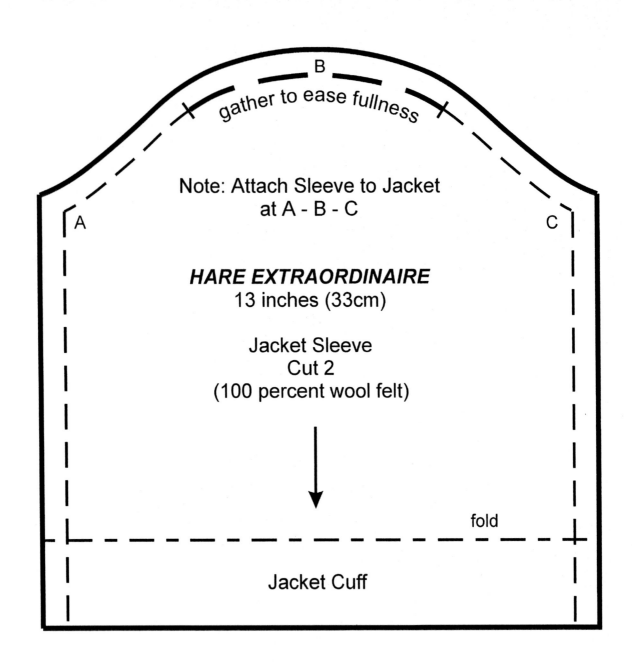
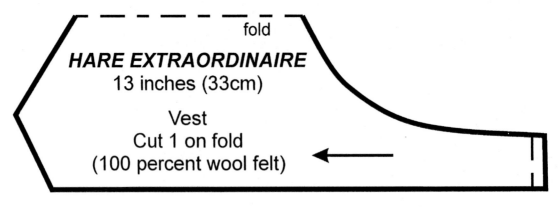

Illustration 14. Pattern Sheet 4 of 7

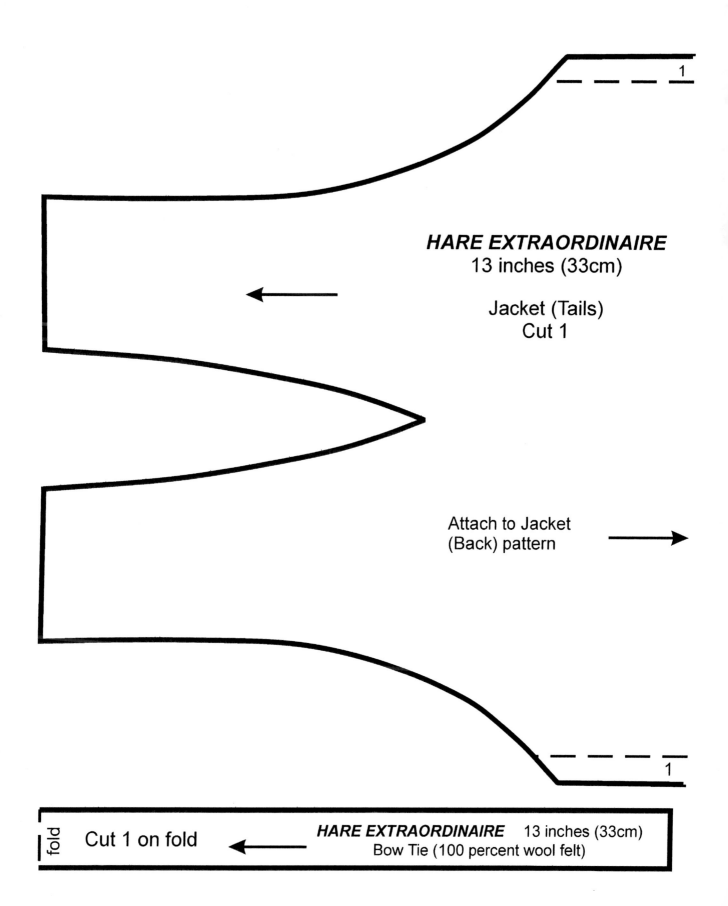

Illustration 15. Pattern Sheet 5 of 7

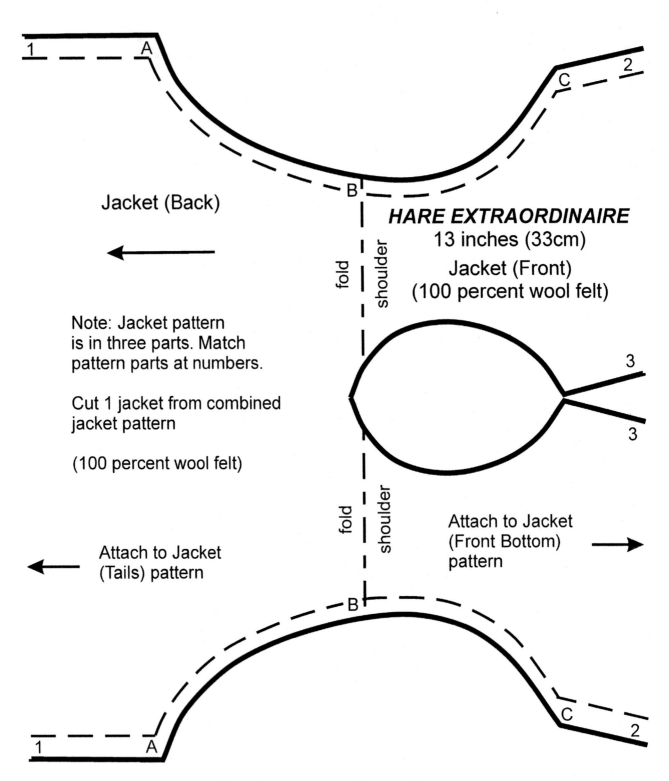

Illustration 16. Pattern Sheet 6 of 7

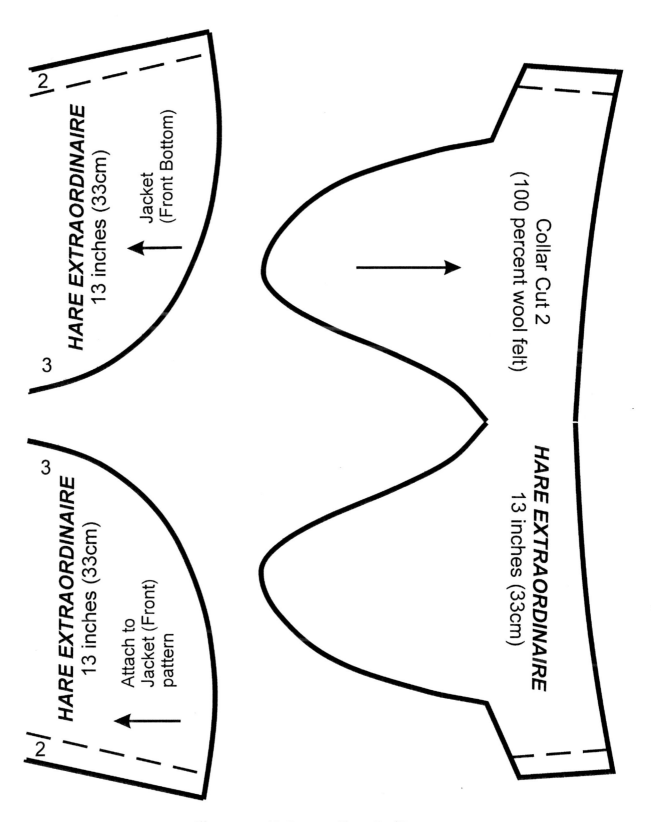

Illustration 17. Pattern Sheet 7 of 7

HEDGEHOG
Size: 6 inches (15cm) – Beginning Level

MATERIALS:

7 inch x 9 inch (18cm x 22cm) square of light, long mohair for head
5 inch (12cm) square of upholstery fabric for ears and base
Two 6mm eyes, glass or plastic
Small amount of fiberfill
Black Perlé cotton thread for embroidering nose
Upholstery thread for attaching eyes and closing seams
Sewing machine thread, color to match fur

This diagram represents all the pieces required to complete the *Hedgehog*, laid out on the straight of the fabric. More than one piece of fabric may be required for laying out the pattern pieces.

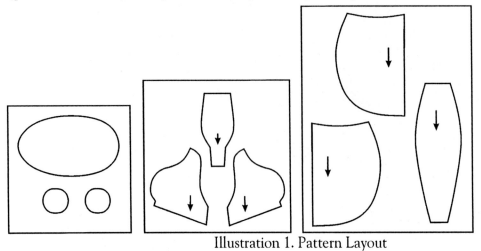

Illustration 1. Pattern Layout

INSTRUCTIONS:

Sew the center head gusset to the side head pieces. Pin the gusset to the side head before sewing, to keep the pieces from moving. Sew the two side head pieces together from the nose down to the neck edge.

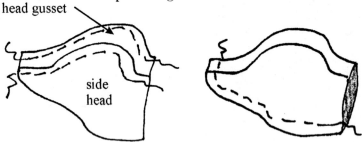

Illustration 2. Sew the Head

Sew the body gusset to the body. Cut a piece of cardboard the size of the base (for stuffing, later). Sew the base to the body, leaving the front open to attach the head.

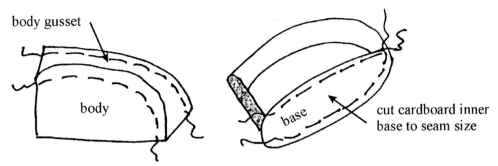

Illustration 3. Sew the Body

Turn both the head and the body. Sew the head to the body from one side to the other across the top. Leave an opening around the base to insert the cardboard inner base.

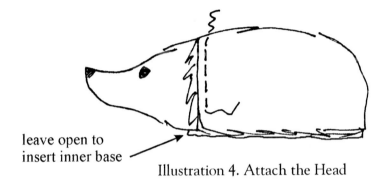

Illustration 4. Attach the Head

Fold and sew the ears. Cut a slit along the fold in order to turn.

Illustration 5. Sew Ears

Insert the cardboard inner base into the body. Stuff and close the seam at the base. Shave the muzzle. Attach the eyes. Attach the ears about 3/4 inch (2cm) behind the eyes. Embroider the nose.

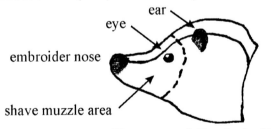

Illustration 6. Finish the Face

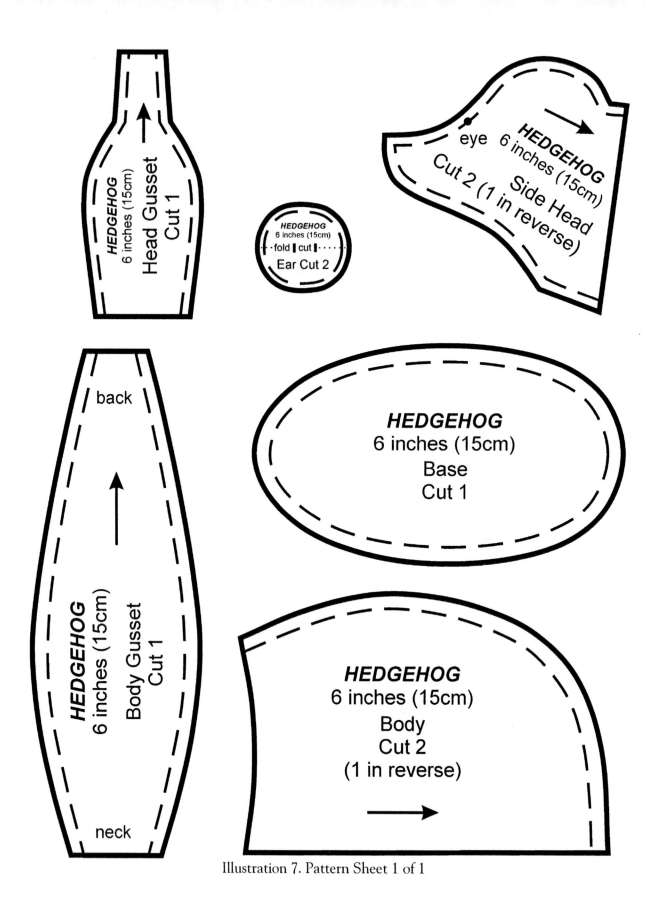

Illustration 7. Pattern Sheet 1 of 1

MONKEY
Size: 16 inches (40cm) – Advanced Level

MATERIALS:

1/2 yard (50cm) of 1 inch (2cm) mohair for body
15 inch (10cm) square of 100 percent wool felt for face, hands, feet and tail
Two 8mm eyes, glass or plastic
Ten 1 1/2 inch (4cm) fiber disks for joints
Five 1 1/2 inch (4cm) cotter pins
Fifteen 1/2 inch (2cm) fender washers
One 16 ounce bag of fiberfill
Perlé cotton thread, dark brown, for embroidering nose and mouth
Nylon thread for attaching eyes and closing seams
Sewing machine thread, color to match fur

This diagram represents all the pieces required to complete the *Monkey*, laid out on the straight of the fabric. More than one piece of fabric may be required for laying out the pattern pieces.

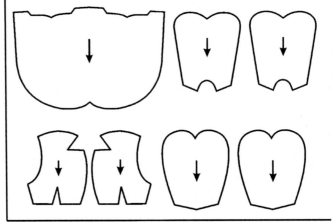

Illustration 1. Pattern Layout

INSTRUCTIONS:

Sew the darts in the two side head pieces.

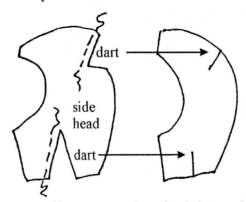

Illustration 2. Sew the Side Head Pieces

Sew the face dart and attach the lower jaw. Sew the face section to the side heads.

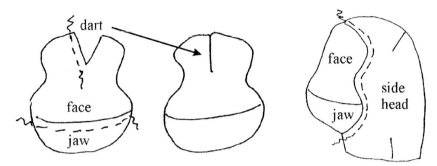

Illustration 3. Sew the Face

Fold the body in half and sew the side seams. Open the body and refold, matching the shoulder seams. Sew the shoulder seams.

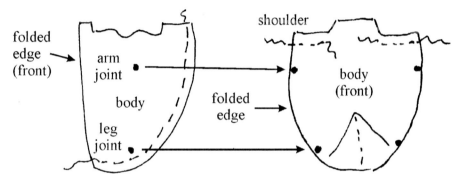

Illustration 4. Sew the Body

Fold the darts in the arm pieces and sew. Sew the hands to the arms. Fold the arms and sew, leaving the top

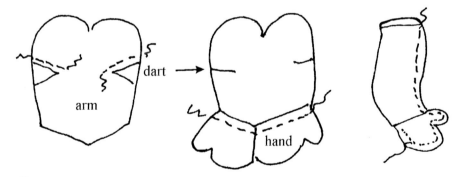

open for stuffing.

Illustration 5. Sew the Arms

Fold the darts in the leg pieces and sew. Fold the legs and sew, leaving the top open for stuffing.

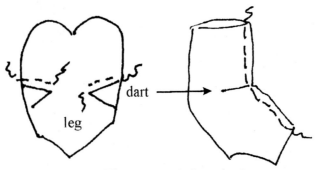

Illustration 6. Sew the Legs

Sew the foot top to the foot bottom around the toes from A to B. Attach the foot to the leg. Sew from A to C to B, then around the back of the foot from B to D and back to A.

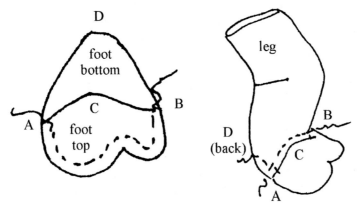

Illustration 7. Sew the Feet

Turn all the pieces. Make up the part of the joint inside the head (washer on cotter pin, fender washer and fiber disk). Stuff and close the head around the disk. Attach the eyes and embroider the nose. Stitch the mouth about 1/2 inch (1cm) above the seam.

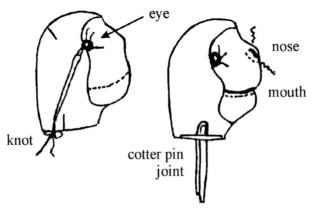

Illustration 8. Complete the Face

Sew the ears together. Turn the ears and topstitch around the outer edge. Attach the ears to the head with a gather to make wrinkles.

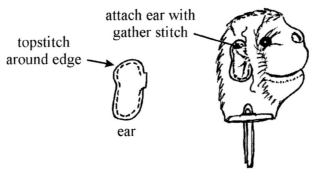

Illustration 9. Attach the Ears

Gather and close the body at the neck. Join the head to the body. Join the arms and legs. Stuff the arms, legs and body. Close the seams.

Fold the tail and sew. Turn, stuff and attach the tail to the body.

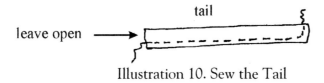

Illustration 10. Sew the Tail

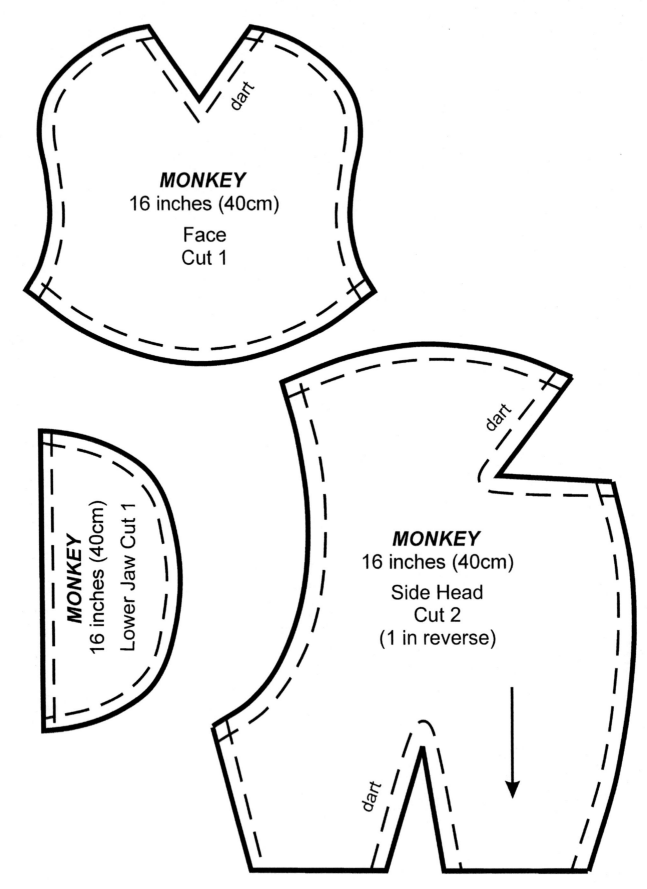

Illustration 11. Pattern Sheet 1 of 4

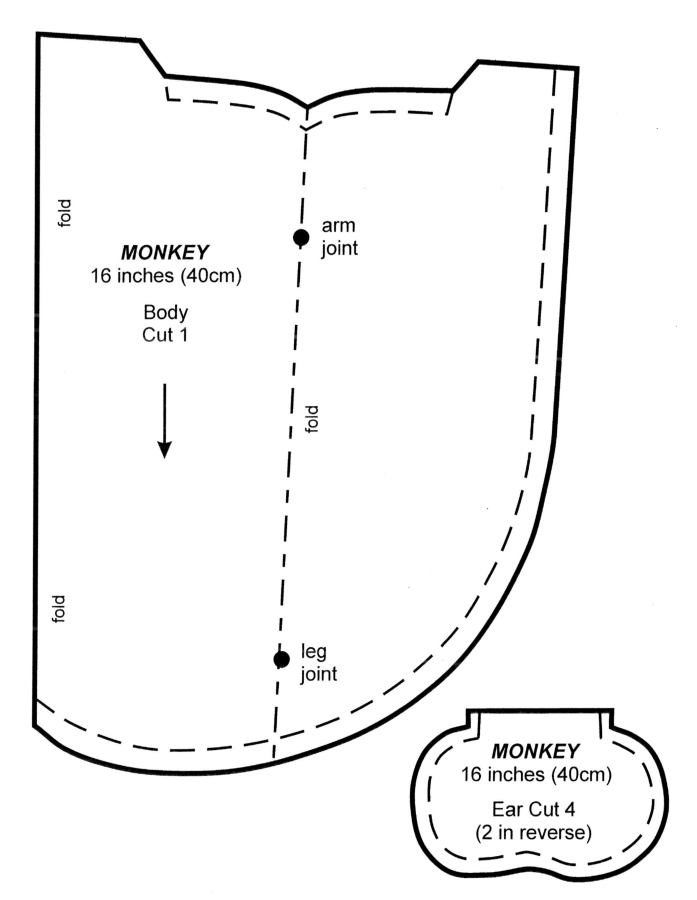

Illustration 12. Pattern Sheet 2 of 4

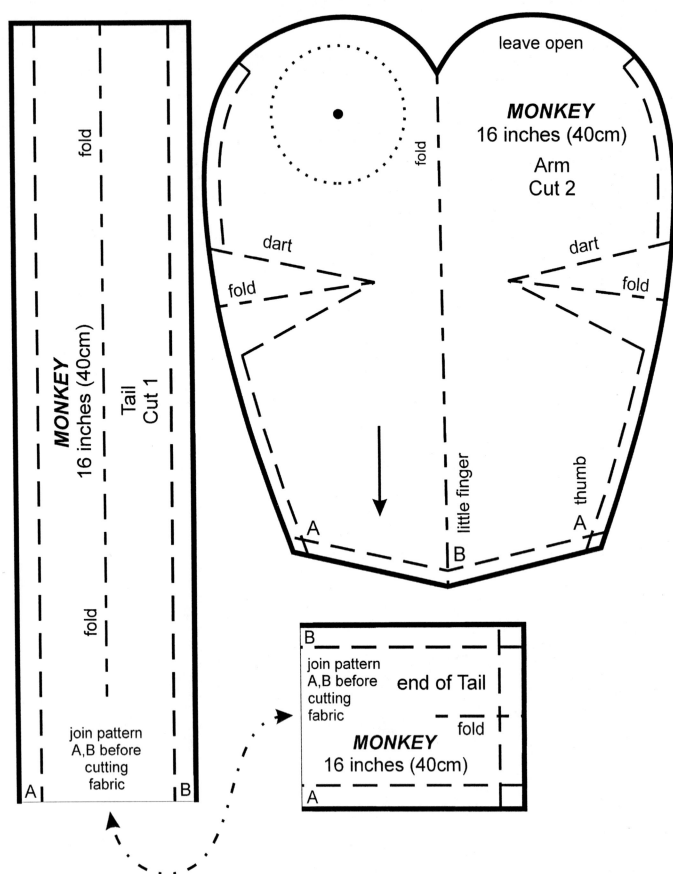

Illustration 13. Pattern Sheet 3 of 4

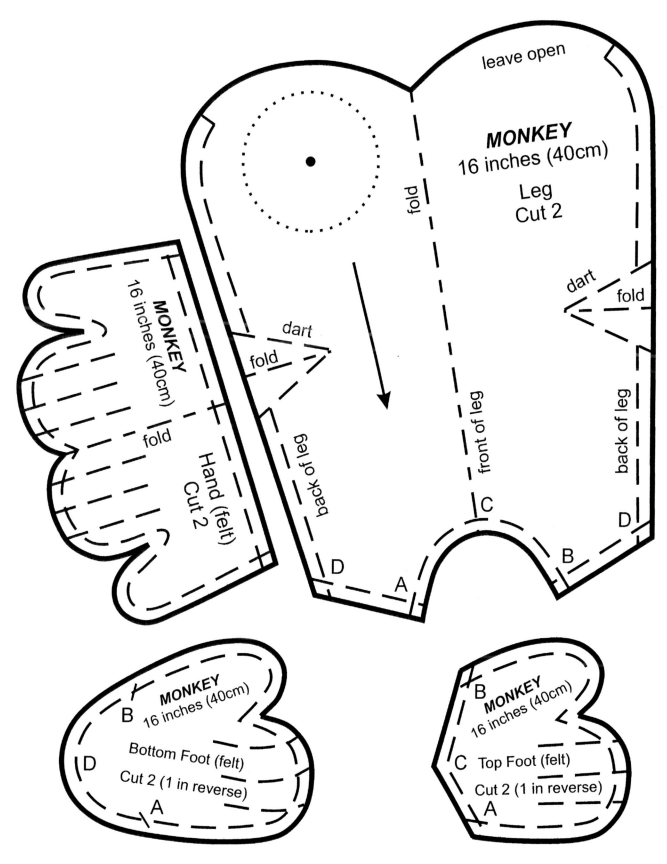

Illustration 14. Pattern Sheet 4 of 4

MOUSE
Size: 10 inches (25cm) – Beginner Level

MATERIALS:

1/4 yard (25cm) of 1/8 inch (.31cm) mohair or upholstery fabric
12 inch (30cm) square of upholstery fabric with nap for feet, paws, ear lining, soles
Two 7mm eyes, glass or plastic
Ten 1 1/2 inch (4cm) diameter fiber disks
Five 1 1/2 inch (4cm) cotter pins
Fifteen 1/2 inch (1cm) fender washers
One 16 ounce bag of fiberfill
Black Perlé cotton thread for mouth
Pink Perlé cotton thread for nose
Upholstery thread for attaching eyes and closing seams
Sewing machine thread, color to match fur
Fabric paint markers for accenting face and ears (dark for inner ear, light for face muzzle)

This diagram represents all the pieces required to complete the *Mouse*, laid out on the straight of the fabric. More than one piece of fabric may be required for laying out the pattern pieces.

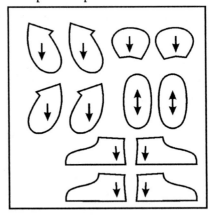

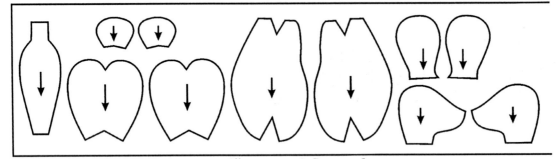

Illustration 1. Pattern Layout

INSTRUCTIONS:

Sew the side heads to the head center gusset. Sew the side heads together from the nose to the neck edge.

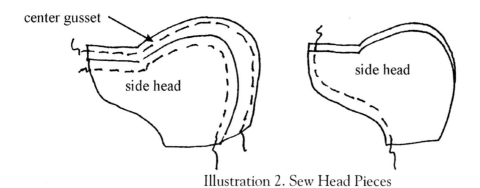

Illustration 2. Sew Head Pieces

Sew the ear and lining together for both ears, leaving the bottom open for turning.

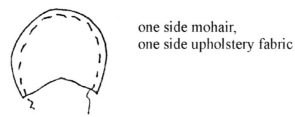

one side mohair,
one side upholstery fabric

Illustration 3. Sew the Ears

Sew the darts in the body pieces. Join the body together, leaving an opening in the back for stuffing.

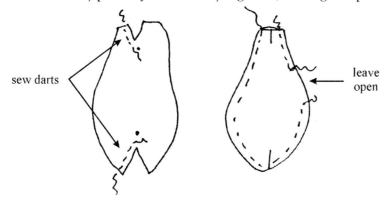

Illustration 4. Sew the Body

Sew the paws to the arms. Fold the arms and sew, leaving the top open for stuffing. Make sure there is a right and left arm.

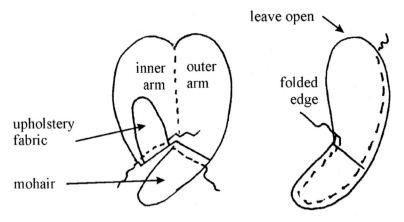

Illustration 5. Sew the Arms

Sew the feet to the legs. Sew legs together, leaving the top open for stuffing. Baste the sole to the bottom of the leg then machine sew the sole to the leg.

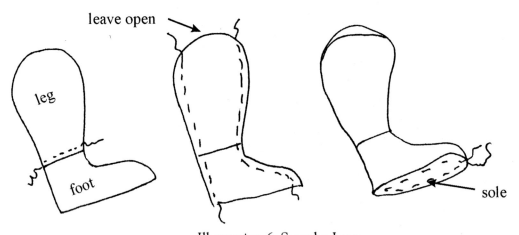

Illustration 6. Sew the Legs

Fold and sew the tail. Leave one end open for turning.

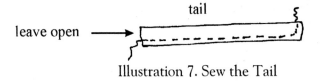

Illustration 7. Sew the Tail

Refer to the **Basic Directions** for finishing the head (stuff, close the neck around the joint disk, attach ears, embroider nose and mouth). Attach the head, arms and legs to the body. Stuff the body. Lightly stuff the fingers and toes of the limbs. Hand stitch the fingers and toes. Then complete stuffing the arms and legs.

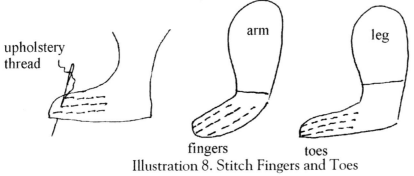

Illustration 8. Stitch Fingers and Toes

Close all seams. Turn the tail and attach to the back body seam.

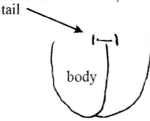

Illustration 9. Attach the Tail

Attach whiskers to the head.

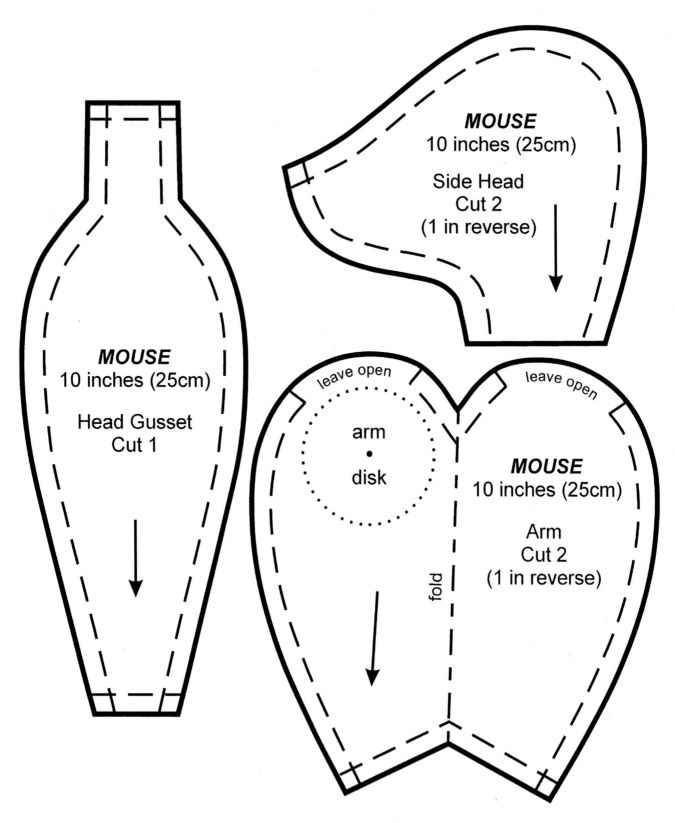

Illustration 10. Pattern Sheet 1of 3

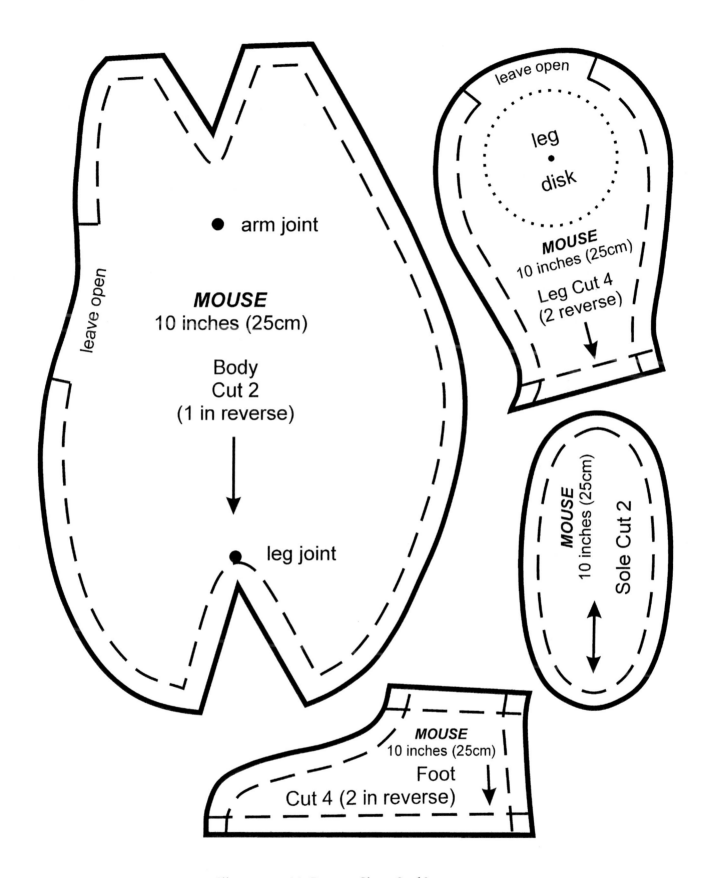
Illustration 11. Pattern Sheet 2 of 3

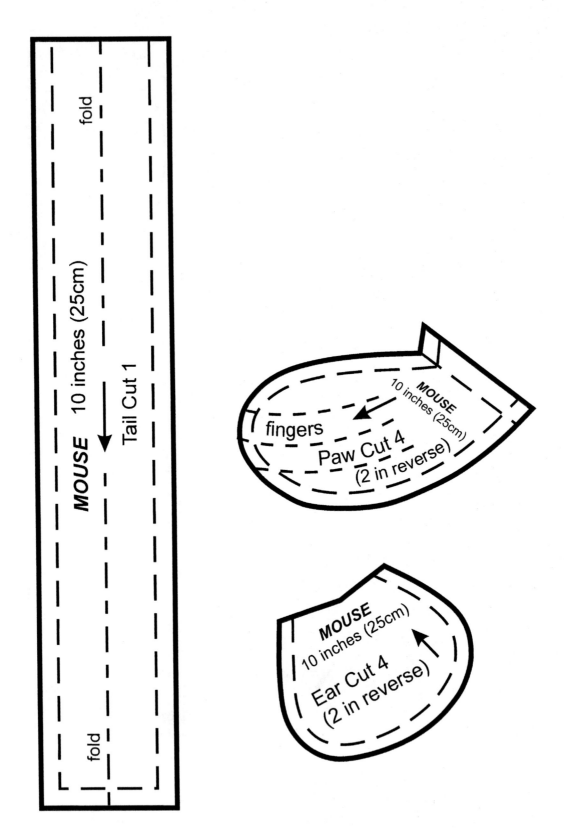

Illustration 12. Pattern Sheet 3 of 3

PANDA
Size: 16 inches (40cm) – Intermediate Level

MATERIALS:

1/4 yard (25cm) each of light and dark mohair (black/white, brown/beige) for body
6 inch x 15 inch (15cm x 40cm) piece of black 100 percent wool felt or upholstery material for paws, soles
Two 8mm eyes, glass or plastic
Eight 2 1/2 inch (6cm) fiber disks for arm, leg joints
Two 3 1/4 inch (8cm) fiber disks for head joint
Ten 1/2 inch (1cm) fender washers
Five sets 1 1/2 inch (4cm) hex head bolts and lock nuts
One 20 ounce bag of fiberfill
Black Perlé cotton thread for embroidering nose and mouth
Upholstery thread for attaching eyes and closing seams
Sewing machine thread, color to match fur
Ribbon or ruffle for decorating

This diagram represents all the pieces required to complete the *Panda,* laid out on the straight of the fabric. More than one piece of fabric may be required for laying out the pattern pieces.

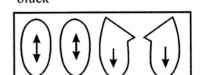

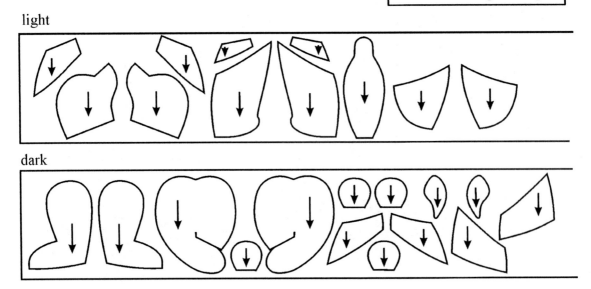

Illustration 1. Pattern Layout

INSTRUCTIONS:

Sew the two side head pieces together from the nose down to the neck edge. Pin the gusset to the side head before sewing, to keep the pieces from moving. Sew the center head gusset to the side head pieces. Sew the ears together.

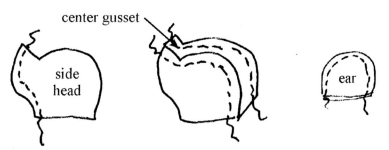

Illustration 2. Sew the Head

Sew the three pieces of the body fronts together. Sew the three pieces of the body backs together.

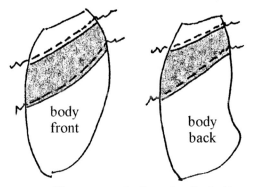

Illustration 3. Sew the Body Pieces

Sew the two halves of the body front together along the front, matching the stripes. Sew the two halves of the body back together, leaving an opening for stuffing. Sew the body front to the body back along the sides, matching the stripes. Leave the neck edge open.

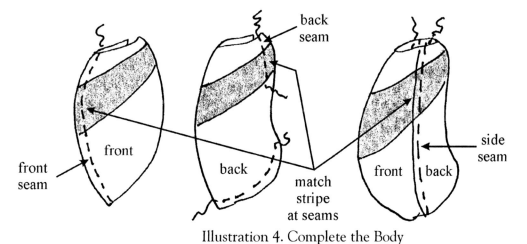

Illustration 4. Complete the Body

Sew the paw to the arm. Fold the arm and sew, leaving the top open for stuffing.

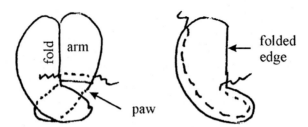

Illustration 5. Sew the Arms

Sew the legs together, leaving the top open for stuffing. Sew the soles.

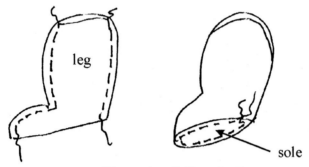

Illustration 6. Sew the Legs

Stuff the head and close around the fiber disk for the head joint (the larger disk). Make a hole in the eye patch and insert the eye. Attach the eyes to the head. Rotate the eye patches into position and sew the patches to the head. Attach the ears.

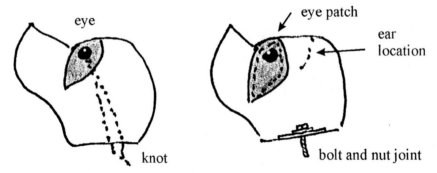

Illustration 7. Attach Eyes and Ears

Shave the muzzle and, if desired, lightly paint. Light brown looks good on a brown and cream colored panda. Embroider the nose and mouth.

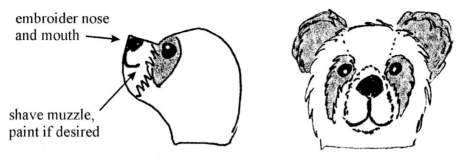

Illustration 8. Complete the Head

Gather the neck of the body. Attach the head. Attach the arms and legs. Stuff and close.

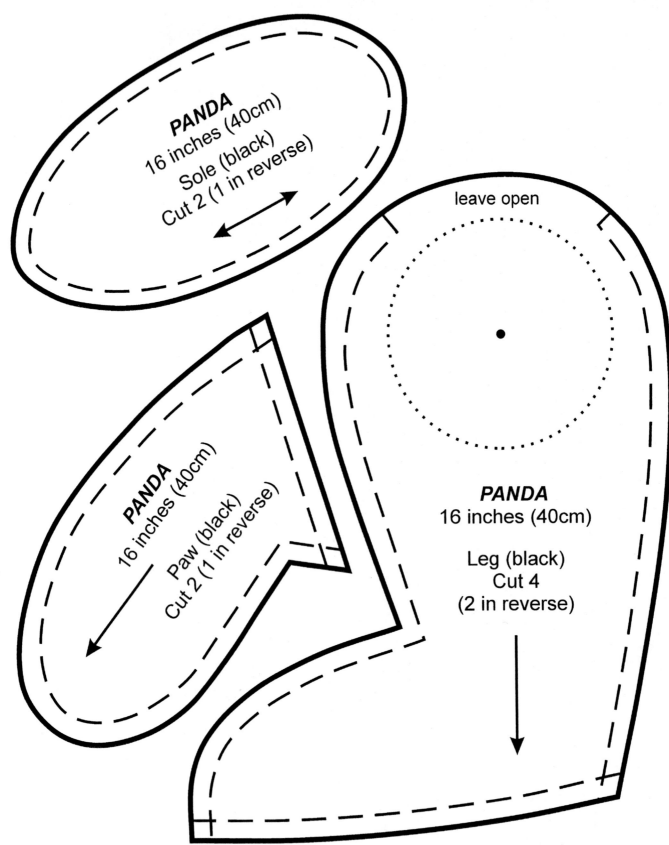

Illustration 9. Pattern Sheet 1 of 6

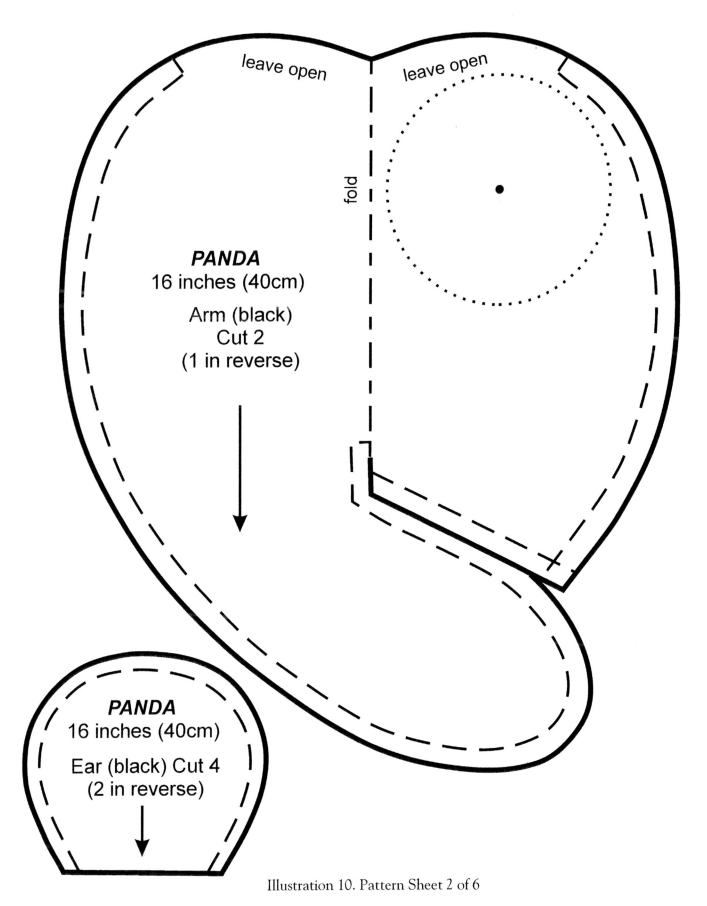

Illustration 10. Pattern Sheet 2 of 6

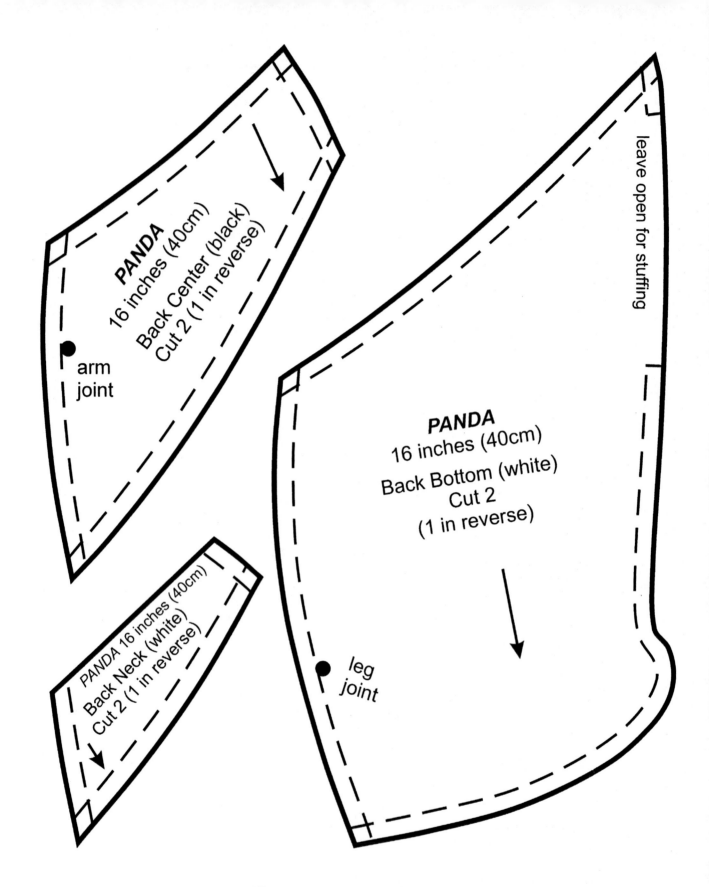

Illustration 11. Pattern Sheet 3 of 6

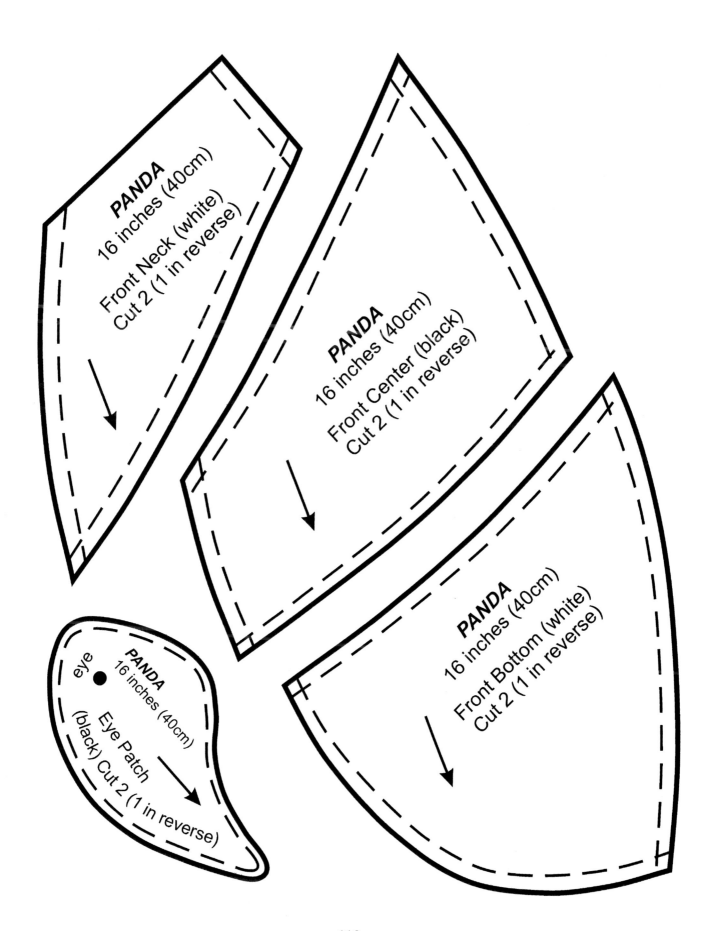

Illustration 12. Pattern Sheet 4 of 6

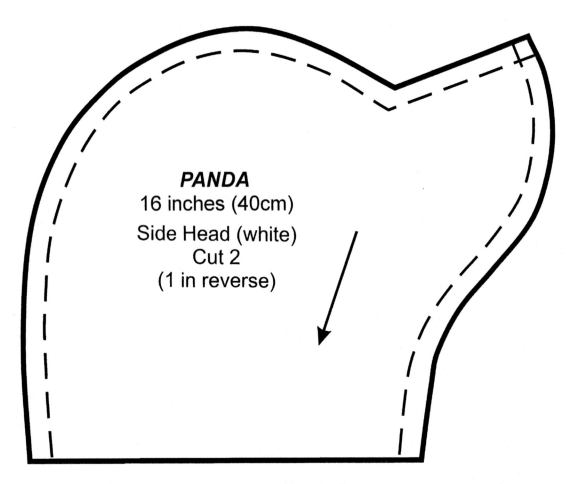

Illustration 13. Pattern Sheet 5 of 6

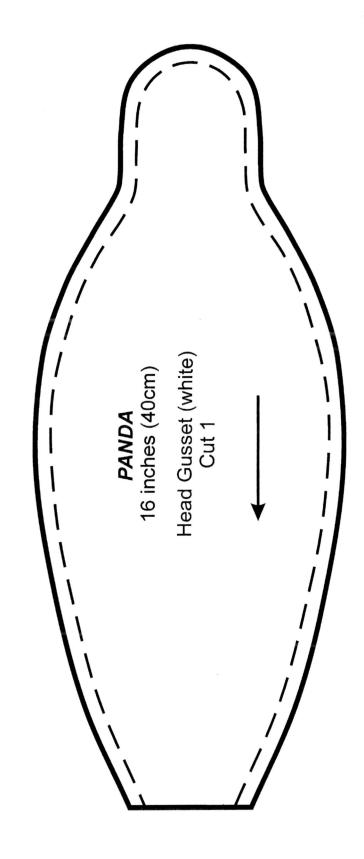

Illustration 14. Pattern Sheet 6 of 6

RAT
Size: 9 inches (23cm) sitting – Intermediate Level

MATERIALS:

1/3 yard (33cm) of 1/8 inch mohair
8 inch x 12 inch (20cm x 30cm) upholstery fabric for ear lining, tail and soles
Two 6mm eyes, glass or plastic
Ten 1 1/2 inch (4cm) fiber disks
Fifteen 1/2 inch (1cm) diameter fender washers
Five 1 1/2 inch (4cm) cotter pins
One 16 ounce bag of fiberfill
Small amount of plastic pellets for weight
Black Perlé cotton thread for embroidering nose
Upholstery thread for attaching eyes and closing seams
Sewing machine thread, color to match fur

This diagram represents all the pieces required to complete the *Rat*, laid out on the straight of the fabric. More than one piece of fabric may be required for laying out the pattern pieces.

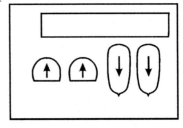

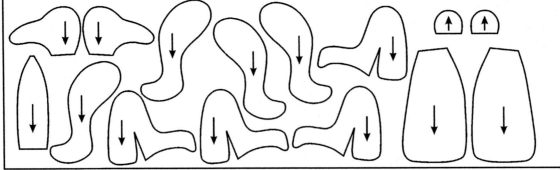

Illustration 1. Pattern Layout

INSTRUCTIONS:

Sew the two side head pieces together from point A down to the neck edge. Sew the head gusset to the side head pieces. Pin the gusset to the side head before sewing to keep the pieces from moving.

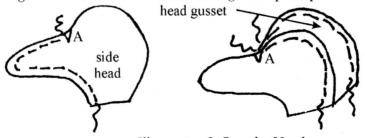

Illustration 2. Sew the Head

Sew the two body pieces together, leaving the back open for stuffing. Sew the ears together.

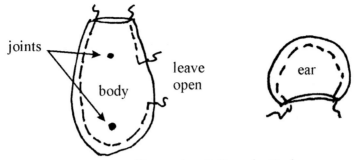

Illustration 3. Sew the Body

Sew the arms together, leaving the top open for stuffing. Sew the legs together, leaving the knee and the foot area at the bottom of the leg open. Sew the soles to the bottom of the feet.

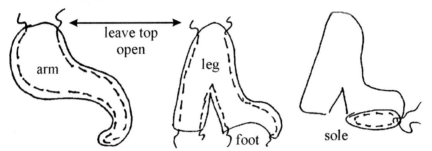

Illustration 4. Sew the Arms and Legs

Fold the tail in half and sew, leaving the tail open for turning and stuffing.

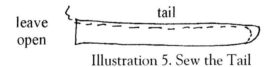

Illustration 5. Sew the Tail

Stuff the head and close around the fiber disk of the head joint. Embroider the nose. Attach the eyes. Gather the ears and attach. Shave the muzzle as shown on the pattern.

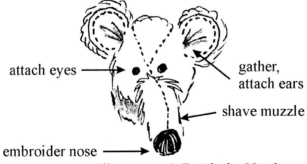

Illustration 6. Finish the Head

Gather and close the body neck. Attach the head to the body. Attach the arms and legs. Stuff the arms, legs and body. Close all seams. Attach the tail. Shave the arms and legs.

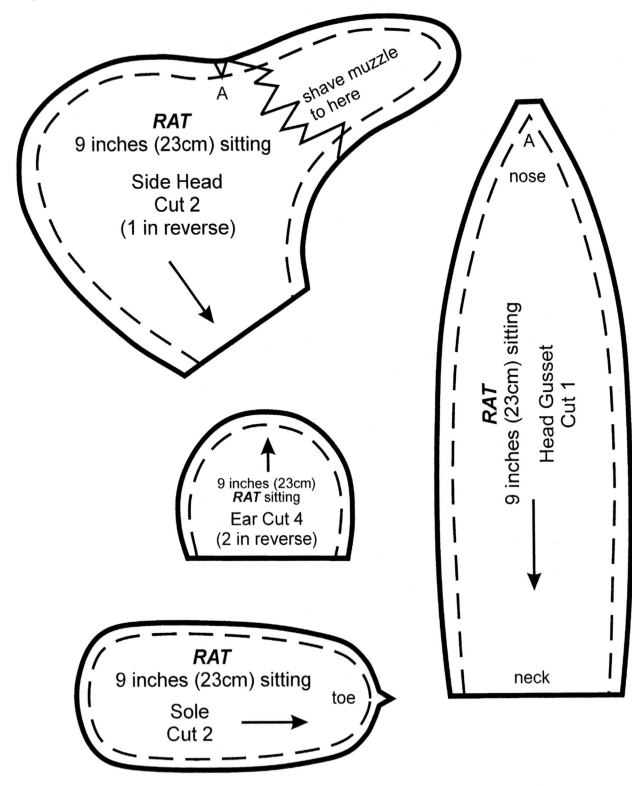

Illustration 7. Pattern Sheet 1 of 3

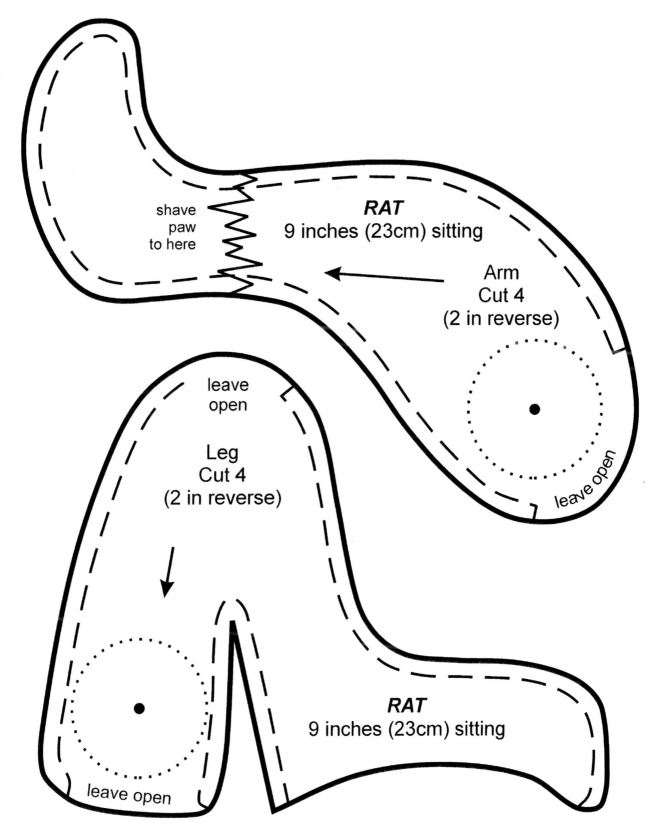

Illustration 8. Pattern Sheet 2 of 3

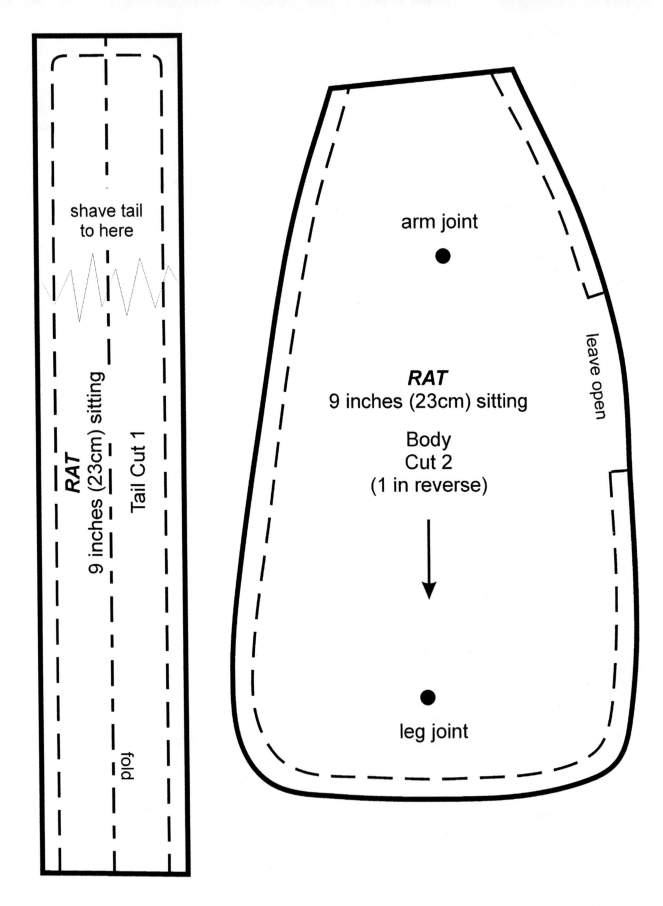

Illustration 9. Pattern Sheet 3 of 3

SOURCES:

United States

Central Shippee, Inc.
46 Star Lake Road
Bloomingdale, NJ 07403 0135
Telephone: 800 631 8968
Website: www.centralshippee.com
100 percent wool felt

Edinburgh Imports, Inc.
PO Box 340
Newbury Park, CA 91319 0340
Telephone: 805 376 1700
Fax: 805 376 1711
Website: www.edinburgh.com

Intercal Trading Group
1760 Monrovia Avenue, Suite A 17
Costa Mesa, CA 92627
Telephone: 949 645 9396
Fax: 949 645 5471
Website: www.intercaltg.com

Canada

Bear Ingredients
588 Edward Ave, Unit 52
Richmond Hill, Ontario
Canada LAC 9Y6
Telephone: 905 770 3173
Fax: 905 770 6811
Website: www.bearingredients.com
E mail: info@bearingredients.com

Bears & Bedtime
4812 50 Ave
Stony Plain, Alberta
Canada T7Z 1S8
Telephone: 780 963 6300;
Toll free: 800 461 BEAR (2327)
Fax: 780 963 2134
Website: www.bearsandbedtime.com
E mail: teddies@bearsandbedtime.com

Disco Joints & Teddies
2 Ridgewood Pl, Box 468
St. Clements, Ontario
Canada NOB 2MO
Telephone: 519 699 4525
Website: www.discojoints.on.ca
E mail: disco@discojoints.on.ca
(Prices are Canadian)

Australia

Beary Cheap Bear Supplies
P O Box 2465
Burleigh, Queensland 4220
Australia
Telephone: 0755 203 455
Fax: 0755 203 411
E mail: sales@bearycheap.com
(Prices are Australian)

Printed in the United Kingdom
by Lightning Source UK Ltd.
107163UKS00001B/3